THE BIG CHILL

Canada and the Cold War

Titles in the *Contemporary Affairs* Series

NUMBER 1
The Big Chill: Canada and the Cold War

NUMBER 2
Knight-Errant? Canada and the Crusade to Ban Anti-Personnel Land Mines

NUMBER 3
Lament for an Army: The Decline of Canadian Military Professionalism

CONTEMPORARY *Affairs* NUMBER 1

THE BIG CHILL

Canada and the Cold War

Robert Bothwell

CANADIAN INSTITUT
INSTITUTE OF CANADIEN DES
INTERNATIONAL AFFAIRES
AFFAIRS INTERNATIONALES

CIIA/ICAI

IRWIN
PUBLISHING

Toronto, Canada

Canadian Cataloguing in Publication Data

Bothwell, Robert, 1944-
   The big chill: Canada and the Cold War

(Contemporary affairs series ; no. 1)
Includes bibliographical references and index.
ISBN 0-7725-2518-8

1. Canada — Foreign relations — 1945-   . 2. Cold War. I. Title. II. Series.

FC602.B67 1997   971.064   C97-932520-X
F1034.2.B67 1997

*The Canadian Institute of International Affairs is a national, non-partisan, non-profit
organization with a mandate to promote the informed discussion, debate and analysis
of foreign policy and international affairs from a Canadian perspective. By virtue of its
constitution, the CIIA is precluded from expressing an institutional opinion on these
issues. The views expressed in the Contemporary Affairs series are, therefore, those of
the author alone.*

Cover Photo: Chris Thomaidis / Tony Stone Images
Design by Sonya V. Thursby / Opus House Incorporated
Typesetting by Opus House Incorporated
Edited by Norma Pettit

Published by
Irwin Publishing
1800 Steeles Avenue West
Concord, ON
L4K 2P3

For my friend
Norman Hillmer

Contents

CONTENTS

Foreword

The Canadian Institute of International Affairs, in cooperation with Irwin Publishing, is very pleased to launch its Contemporary Affairs series of monographs with Robert Bothwell's history of Canada and the Cold War. Professor Bothwell, a much-published author and highly regarded lecturer on Canadian history, foreign affairs and politics, is the Canadian expert on this subject, and his monograph surveys a huge field while adding new information and a challenging interpretation.

Canadians are used to thinking of themselves as a small nation of relatively little importance in global affairs. The history of the Cold War, however, gives the lie to this too-easy generalization. First, geography unquestionably made Canada important. Then, though it naturally fluctuated over time and circumstance, the Canadian government and people were deeply committed to the democratic cause and the necessity to contain Soviet expansionism. This led Canada to station forces overseas for more than four decades, an unprecedented commitment in our history. It also led to substantial expenditures on defence, again something that had never been the norm in Canada, except in wartime.

The Cold War shaped the post-1945 era. It drove Canada's international relations, it affected our domestic politics, and it had a lasting impact on each and every Canadian. Robert Bothwell's erudite and wise examination of this subject is an essential primer, an object lesson in the ways in which Canada pursued its national interest.

J. L. Granatstein
Rowell Jackman Resident Fellow
Canadian Institute of International Affairs

Introduction

The Cold War, lasting from the end of the Second World War in 1945 until 1991, was a time of illusions. There was, first, the illusion of danger: danger from the East, from the vast and malign Soviet Union and its dupes in the West. There was the illusion of strength: the power of the atomic bomb, and the capacity to destroy the world. There was the illusion of solidarity: East and West, NATO and the Warsaw Pact, alliances whose fate was never to be tested in war. There was the illusion that the Cold War existed out of time, that it would last forever, and that it overshadowed past and present.

Like a mirage, the Cold War fragments and recedes the closer one approaches. The Cold War was not a single seamless unit, but a succession of episodes, of phases. The early Cold War may not even have begun in 1945 but in 1917 with the Russian Revolution. In Canada's case there was a long pre-1945 history of suspicion of radicals with their pockets stuffed with Soviet gold. The triumph of socialism in one country, the Soviet Union, created an impression of strength and power and purpose. In fact, the existence and acceptance of Soviet subsidies, and the subservience of Canada's Communists to Moscow helped to retard and ultimately doom two generations of radicals while often turning much of the Canadian Left into a laughingstock.

The spread of Soviet power into Central and Eastern Europe also created an illusion of solidity and strength. In fact, the existence of a Soviet Empire helped weaken the Soviet Union by draining its strength and confusing its commitments. It also stimulated a reaction from the West, a reaction in which Canada fully shared. Apprehension and at times fear flourished as the Soviet Union completed the communization of Eastern Europe.

Canada became fully committed to the Cold War in 1949-50, with the establishment of NATO and the Korean War. The former provided a paper guarantee of Western Europe, a promissory note that the Canadian government hoped would never be cashed. Korea spurred on Canada's largest peacetime mobilization, tripling the armed forces, over-stimulating the economy, and straining the nation's tolerance of domestic Communists.

The psychological mobilization of the 1950s lasted into the early 1960s; so did the commitment to a big army. The Berlin Crisis of 1958-61 and the Cuban Missile Crisis of October 1962 proved to be turning points. Canadian enthusiasm for the Cold War rapidly decompressed in the 1960s, while Canadian energy and money were diverted to building social security at home rather than national security abroad.

The final phase of the Cold War, from roughly 1968 until the collapse of the Soviet Empire in 1989-91, was sometimes serious enough, but it was a period in which Canada was increasingly distant from its allies. Canadian armed forces were reduced, public attention wandered elsewhere, and Canadians discovered new missions and new objectives, from peacekeeping to pensions. Nevertheless, Canada remained where geography, history and ideology originally placed it, firmly on the Western side in the Cold War.

This small book traces the history of the Cold War, and attempts to explain the twists, turns and apparent inconsistencies of Canada's participation. There is, however, one clear consistency: at no point were Canadians seriously tempted to jump the fence, turn to neutrality or abandon the Western side. Public opinion would not have stood for it; and, as this book suggests, given the nature of the adversary, public opinion was right.

Chapter One

Origins

The Cold War is a term applied to the relations between the democratic countries of North America and Western Europe and the Communist countries of Eastern Europe and Asia. The term was popularized though probably not originated by the American journalist Walter Lippmann in 1947. It seemed so apt that it was immediately adopted around the world to describe the unfriendly relations between the Soviet Union and the Western powers, and it remained in service until the final collapse of the Soviet Union in 1991.

Canada was one of those Western countries that in 1947 found themselves reluctantly confronting the Soviet Union. For the next forty-five years Canada was, in one way or another, caught up in the Cold War. Canadians from the 1940s to the 1990s identified themselves as members of the Western camp, as an integral component of the "Free World," whose leading nation, the United States, was their country's only neighbour.

The Cold War was a matter of overwhelming importance. It affected Canadian life, and Canadian lives, in a thousand different ways. It affected the balance between external and internal policy and politics. Yet it is possible to exaggerate where the Cold War is concerned. Because of its significance, its duration and its effects, it is sometimes treated as if it was always the most important item in Canada's repertoire of foreign policies.

Forty-five years is a long time. Canadian history passed through several cycles of different kinds between 1945 and 1991: periods of prosperity and recession, of integration and devolution, of Baby Boom and Baby Bust, of nationalism and nationalisms. If the Cold War impinged on these events, these events also influenced Canada's participation in the Cold War. A Canadian diplomat once wrote of the early Cold War as a "Time of Fear and Hope." He applied these terms to a limited period, and to foreign policy alone. It is possible to employ these words more broadly. The Fear (of the Soviet Union, of commu-

1

nism, of war) embodied in the Cold War co-existed with the Hope for a more equitable society, in which prosperity both signalled the success of a liberal-democratic society and simultaneously helped shore up its defences against foreign tyranny and domestic discontent.

The Seeds Are Sown

The Fear did not suddenly appear. Like all history, Canada's Cold War had a pre-history. The pre-history went back to the First World War or even further, to the revolutionary socialist movements of the early twentieth century. Confronted by the social and economic inequalities of industrial capitalism in North America and Europe, some idealists and visionaries imagined a better life in a society transformed for the common benefit of all. Some drew the conclusion that such a transformation could only be the fruit of revolution.

Revolutionary socialism was destined to triumph in only one country. The Russian Empire, undermined by war and political incompetence of a truly stunning magnitude, fell into the hands of the Bolshevik ("majority") faction of the Russian Social Democratic Party. The Bolsheviks' ideology was not especially novel—familiar prophecies of a golden socialist future—but their tactics were direct and effective. Relying on an elite revolutionary minority, they were not troubled by considerations of democratic politics or lack of electoral support. The Bolsheviks, or Communists as they became known, suppressed any and all opposition to their regime. Ruling in the name of the people, they found it unnecessary to consult the people or to take them seriously—except in the abstract.

The Communists' great strength, their readiness to use force to achieve their ends, was also their weakness. Once they had come to rely on violence they found it very difficult to let go of such a handy instrument. Their reluctance was even greater when it became obvious that they could not implement their economic program of state control and ownership of all sectors of the economy without relying on, first, intimidation and then, terror.

The Bolsheviks, under their leader V.I. Lenin, seized power in Russia in November 1917. In January 1918 they negotiated a truce with the Germans, and in March a treaty of peace, ending Russia's participation in the First World War. Russia's former allies, Great Britain, France and the United States, took a dim view of these proceedings, which confirmed their repugnance for the form and content of Lenin's politics. Hoping to return Russia to the war against Germany and coincidentally suppress communism, the allies sent small bodies of troops and large quantities of supplies to the fringes of the former Russian Empire where some anti-Communist Russians had gathered to mount an opposition to the Communists. This policy was appropriately called Intervention.

Canadian troops happened to be available for Intervention, one group in north Russia, and another in Siberia. They did little good in north Russia and in Siberia little at all. Both the Canadian government and public opinion in Canada saw Intervention as a part of the war against Germany and not as the first shot in a universal crusade against communism, and in 1919, after the collapse of the German enemy, the government called its troops home. Sir Robert Borden, the Canadian prime minister (1911-20), once asked a Canadian colonel with experience in Russia what it would take to suppress bolshevism. A million men, was the enthusiastic reply—probably an accurate estimate. The Canadian government was not up for that, and neither were the leaders of Great Britain, the United States and France. Intervention was terminated, and the incompetence of Russia's domestic anti-Communists gave Lenin and his followers the victory they had been seeking. The Red Army decimated its opposition, imposing Communist rule wherever it travelled. By late 1920 the Communists were the unconditional masters of Russia, but of Russia alone. No other country had followed the Russian example. This was a surprise and a disappointment to Russia's Communist rulers who believed, as a matter of faith and principle, that revolution must be universal.

Communist Russia soon became the Union of Soviet Socialist Republics, or Soviet Union, a sham federation of Communist "states," united in strict subordination to Moscow and to the Communist regime that took up residence in Moscow's Kremlin. For the next seventy years the doings of "the Kremlin," or the policies of "the USSR" or "Soviet Union" occupied the nomenclature of international politics. We shall follow the custom of the period in which for most purposes except anachronism or history, Russia was the Soviet Union and Russians were (in English at least) "the Soviets."

The Soviet Union was a distant country, even if, theoretically, its Arctic Ocean frontier bordered Canada's. There was no danger of the Red Army marching across the ice floes. Canada, like the rest of the British Empire, recognized the Soviet Union in the 1920s and received a Soviet trade mission in Montreal. This mission was not a normal consulate. It dispensed counterfeit Canadian dollars and boxes of anti-capitalist propaganda along with trade, and so was closed by an indignant but unsurprised Canadian government. As a result, Canada had no formal relations with the Soviet Union

3

through the 1930s until the Second World War.

Neither country felt the lack acutely. In the booming 1920s Canada had no need of Soviet trade. In the economically depressed 1930s, Canada's main official concern about the Soviet Union was that the Soviet Union's exports of timber, minerals, and furs competed with Canadian exports. The Soviets saw Canada in more theoretical terms, as contested ground between two empires, the declining British and the rising American. These trends gave hope to Communists everywhere, who believed, as a matter of faith, that capitalists inevitably fell to quarrelling over their economic spoils. Canada was thus an object of struggle, and not a subject of policy, since in the Soviet scheme of things a small intermediate place like Canada could not hope to have an independent policy about anything. Traces of this point of view lingered, and could still be found in Soviet commentaries of the 1980s.

Contacts were not limited to trade or ideology. Thousands of former Russians, immigrants before and after the First World War, lived in Canada, but they were ethnically diverse and politically contradictory. Although there were certainly immigrants from the former Russian Empire such as the "Red Finns" and certain left-wing Ukrainians who sympathized with Lenin and communism, they were politically marginal.

The same could be said of the Canadian Communist party, which was cobbled together out of the fragments of several older, radical and socialist movements in 1921. There is no doubt that the party enjoyed roots that were authentically Canadian. There is equally no doubt that very early in its existence the party fell under the dominance of its Soviet model.

That model was in the 1920s becoming increasingly authoritarian. Lenin tolerated no opposition of any kind outside the party, and very little inside. Secret police and concentration camps were a feature of Soviet rule, and the Communist leadership demonstrated an early fondness for the firing squad. When Lenin died in 1924 the general secretary of the Soviet Communist party, Joseph Stalin, soon took his place, eliminating his rivals in several stages and purges.

The Communist parties of the world were united in a "Communist International" or Comintern. Like the Soviet Union, the Comintern was theoretically a federation of equal parties; and like the Soviet Union, federation and equality were the merest fig-leaf of a sham. By the end of the 1920s, the Comintern was a chorus singing revolutionary hymns to their revolutionary idol, Stalin. It did not hurt that Stalin was also their paymaster, and that Soviet gold flowed in regular transfusions into the veins of Communist parties overseas.

Technically, Stalin was not the head of the Soviet state, but merely the pope of the Communist parties at home and abroad. Realistically, his word was absolute from the Baltic to the Pacific and, through his secret agents, in much of the rest of the world too. Much time was wasted in the 1920s and later "proving" that communism and the Communist party were not one and the same thing as the government of the Soviet Union and that Stalin was some kind of political abstraction dwelling on the sidelines of life. In practice, Stalin and the Soviet state and the Communist party were joined at the hip.

Because of Stalin's importance as absolute boss of the Soviet Communist party and leader of the Soviet state, as well as supreme arbiter and fund-raiser for Communists around the world, his personality and his conception of international relations mattered. Few if any Canadians ever were admitted to Stalin's presence, but there are plenty of descriptions of Stalin's personality and views from other foreigners, and, of course, from Soviet citizens, from the 1920s on.

As an orthodox Communist, Stalin believed in the inevitability of world revolution; yet he had scant personal background or knowledge for assessing events or trends abroad. Unlike other Soviet leaders of the period, such as Lenin or his arch-rival Leon Trotsky, he was not well travelled nor especially well read on non-Russian or non-Marxist subjects. However, Stalin did not achieve his position as leader of the Soviet Union without notable qualities. Two recent Russian historians write of his "dark mind—powerful, willful, suspicious, vindictive."[1] He had a prodigious memory and an ability to take swift and decisive action while his rivals and colleagues were mulling over what they should do.

In the 1930s Stalin confirmed his supremacy inside the Soviet Union by shooting or otherwise disposing of his rivals, real or imagined, in the famous "purges." He crushed resistance among the peasantry—the large majority of the Soviet population—by deporting or starving or murdering literally millions. He forced his country into a crash course in industrialization designed to make the Soviet Union an economic great power along the lines of the United States.

Stalin collectivized Soviet agriculture. He devised "Five-Year Plans" that established and then quickly expanded a "command economy." The term means what it says, commands issued and implemented. Power stations mushroomed, factories were founded, and industry boomed. The Plans seemed rational, even if they could only be accomplished by force or the threat of force. Perhaps that was

5

what was needed to bring a stubborn peasant population into the twentieth century, Western sympathizers argued. Perhaps the purges really were necessary. Perhaps the Soviet Union really was a unique experiment, to be protected, rationalized, justified.

Stalin's country paid an awful price for his achievement. Yet Stalin's policies had a monstrous grandeur that attracted as many as they repelled. It is indisputable that idealists outside the Soviet Union admired Stalin's achievements, and saw in them hope and purpose at a time when the Western capitalist world seemed to be on the verge of chaos or worse.

The economic crisis of the 1930s, the Great Depression, devastated the Western democracies, sapping their political will and creating a demand, especially on the part of youth, for action. In Germany, the Depression led to the fall of the democratic parties and the rise to power of Adolf Hitler and his Nazis. In Great Britain and France, the pillars of international order after 1919, the Depression fed a crisis of nerves, as governments fixated on their depleted financial balance sheets and asked themselves what they could do next. In the United States it led to the election of Democratic politician Franklin D. Roosevelt as president in 1932, and to Roosevelt's inspiring if economically muddled New Deal. And in Canada, hard-hit by the Depression but a more conservative and traditional country than the United States, it contributed to a decade of cautious, conservative politics.

Though the Depression of the 1930s is rightly considered a radicalizing and radical decade, radicals from the Left did not achieve power in any Western capitalist country. But radicals on the Left grew in number and influence, in Canada's case especially in the labour movement and among youth. Some expressed their frustration by joining the Communist party of Canada, which had been waiting for just such an event as the Depression to discredit its rivals, both among the capitalist parties and among the democratic socialists who still accepted and cherished the democratic political system. Many people who were not willing to go as far as communism nevertheless admired its idealism and vigour, even the Stalinist kind.

Communism was distinctly a minority taste, but its claim to idealism, its apparent rationality, and its ability to secure results, to get things done, had a wider appeal. Ordinary politicians, in Canada and elsewhere, worried and sometimes passed laws to turn back the Red tide. For a time in the 1930s Canadian laws banned communism and imprisoned its leaders. Quebec, under a conservative-nationalist government, closed and "padlocked" all premises used for "Communist" meetings. (The definition of "communism" was in practice left to the police.)

Communists were denounced as agents and hirelings of the Soviet government—with some truth in some cases, as we now know. What politicians were worried about was not Soviet aggression or espionage; Canada, virtually disarmed, had no military secrets and even fewer non-military ones. Rather, politicians feared domestic revolution on the Soviet model. Business and most churches (and especially the Roman Catholic Church) were actively anti-Communist. In Roman Catholic Quebec, anti-communism was especially fervent and politically potent. Ironically, in bilingual Montreal, there were a fair number of Communists, as there were in other large Canadian cities.

Communists in Canada and elsewhere understood that their best bet was to infiltrate sympathetic organizations such as student groups, or trade unions. By using tactical political skills honed over years of struggle, they could often succeed in taking over the leadership of such organizations, shaping them to their purpose. In the later 1930s, this approach fitted in with the approved Soviet strategy of the "Popular Front," the anti-fascist union of liberals and leftists to resist fascism and Nazism.

Sometimes, perhaps often, the tactic worked as prescribed. Sometimes it worked the other way. Communists could take power and hold power in trade unions, but often only as long as they served the purposes of the members. These purposes were usually economic, including improved wages and working conditions. Converting these aims into support for world revolution was not easy, and sometimes downright impossible.

The Second World War

The crisis of capitalism in the 1930s was parallelled by a crisis in international order, as the principal loser of the First World War, Germany, prepared to reclaim what had been lost, and more. The German Nazi party was officially anti-Communist, though Communists and Nazis could sometimes make a comfortable transition from one radical movement to another. Nazism preached the supremacy of one nation, Germany, and a strictly graded hierarchy of other peoples down to the arch-enemy, the Jews. Communism was free of this particular excrescence, though there was much else in its brutal practice that the Nazis could admire.

At first Nazi Germany and the Soviet Union functioned as rivals, and Stalin sought to create an anti-Nazi coalition against Adolf Hitler. The Western powers, Britain and France, dithered, while the United States contributed little more than words to support international order. Meanwhile, in the Far East, the Japanese Empire was also seeking to expand, mostly at the expense of China though increasingly, as the decade wore on, at the cost of the Western powers' colonial empires in the region. Japan and Germany were increasingly attracted to one another though they did not formally become allies until 1940, a year after the Second World War finally broke out.

Stalin prepared for the outbreak of the war by making a "Non-Aggression Pact" with Hitler in August 1939. It was a diplomatic coup for Hitler, who could now fight the war he was planning to start with much less risk than before. It was, similarly, a diplomatic disaster for Britain and France, and their ally Poland. Secret provisions in the treaty called for the division of Eastern Europe between Germany and the USSR, and over the next year the Soviet Union acquired the eastern half of Poland, the Baltic States of Estonia, Lithuania and Latvia, and part of Romania. In return Soviet raw materials fed the German war machine.

Communists around the world were instructed to follow the Moscow line. From being militantly anti-Nazi, they suddenly preached benign neutrality where Germany was concerned. If proof were needed that Communist parties around the world were little better than tools of the Soviet leadership, this was it. Many Communists quit the party, rather than oppose the war against Hitler. In Canada and elsewhere, Communists were banned on the outbreak of war, and interned. But in Stalin's calculations, the disaffection and imprisonment of a few Communists was probably a temporary setback, justified by the immense gains of territory and time that he believed he had made.

Stalin was probably counting on a long and costly war between Germany and Britain and France. Hitler upset his calculations by rapidly defeating the allies and occupying all of Western Europe north of the Pyrenees and east of the English Channel. Only Great Britain, supported by its Commonwealth and Empire, including Canada, held out against him. His quick victories in Western Europe gave Hitler the opportunity to turn his attention eastward, and in June 1941 he attacked the Soviet Union with his war machine. The Soviet Union thereby became a reluctant ally of Great Britain and the defeated democracies of Western Europe. When, in December 1941, Japan attacked the American fleet in Pearl Harbor, Hitler obligingly came to the help of his Japanese partner and declared war on the United States. Hitler's declaration created the Grand Alliance of the Western democracies in Second World War, and laid the stage for the ultimate victory of the allies over Germany and Japan.

Canada and the Soviet Union thus became tardy allies. Canada during the war was part arsenal, part recruiting ground. Canadian farms produced wheat and meat, Canadian factories made guns and trucks. Canadian families sent their children to war—a million of them, out of a population of twelve million. With France and the rest of Western Europe under German occupation, Canada was the third-ranking ally on the Western side, after the United States and Great Britain. The three English-speaking powers[2] formed an increasingly cozy relationship on all levels, political, administrative, military and economic.

The United States, Great Britain and Canada gave aid to the Soviet Union. The Soviet Union recognized this fact by establishing an embassy in Ottawa in 1943, and Soviet diplomats and military officers became regular figures on the capital's cocktail and reception circuit, as they pressed for more trucks, more guns, more aid of all kinds. During the war Canada sent almost $160 million worth of aid to the Soviet Union, more than to any other non-British country.[3]

Canadian aid to the Soviet Union, however, created something of a paradox. Canadians were on the whole anti-Communist, distrustful of the Soviet Union. Aid to the Soviet Union had to be justified, not merely on cold strategic grounds, but because the Russians were worthy allies. Previously anti-Communist politicians appealed for help for Russia and lent respectability to Russian aid drives. Yet secret government opinion samples found "latent fears" in English Canada (more overt ones in Roman Catholic French Canada) that "we will have to fight Russia"—a view that according to Canada's Wartime Information Board appeared "with disquieting frequency." Opinion in Canada toward the Soviet Union was consistently more conservative, and more hostile, than opinion in the United States.[4]

Although Canada was the third-ranking Western ally, it was not represented at the higher councils of the allies. Grand strategy was left to the leaders of the three great powers: Roosevelt of the United States, Churchill of Great Britain, and Stalin of the Soviet Union. While victory was still in doubt, or a distant prospect, these three and their advisers had no trouble agreeing. Only in 1943, with German armies in retreat and the Americans steadily advancing in the Pacific against the Japanese, did the question of postwar relationships become a serious issue.

The War Ends

War is usually regarded as an abnormal state, and peace as a natural situation. For the allies of 1943-4, normal or natural meant, most probably, the world of 1938, minus Hitler. If that were so, then the old mistrust between Communists and non-Communists would return. The war would be a temporary detour, necessary but in the final analysis a tangent in the grand march of historical inevitability. To some historians, this pre-existing split between East and West is the true origin of the Cold War.

Yet the war changed many things. In the West, the Second World War ended the Great Depression. There was full employment, in fact labour scarcity, virtually everywhere. The war had enforced co-operation between workers and managers (and ultimately owners) in the interest of a harmonious war effort. The war contributed fundamentally to the health of the states that ran it. In the Western democracies high taxes and government management of the economy encouraged the belief that "planning," a key word of the period, could solve the basic problems of the economy, which, on the level of the individual voter meant security, including predictable jobs, decent wages, and reliable government. A wise government promised all these, and pointed to the record of the war—"full employment"—as proof. Unlike the 1930s, governments understood the economy, or so they believed. And indeed much more was known about the economy, in Canada as elsewhere, at the end of the war than at the beginning. An alternative democratic model to totalitarian communism, with its apparent rationality and penchant for Plans, had been created.[5]

The domestic consequences of war were one thing, and a very important thing. Consequences abroad were something else. On land, the Soviet Union bore the brunt of the war. Hitler threw nine million troops at the Soviet Union, which in 1943-4 threw them back. The Soviet Union suffered greatly during the war, to the tune of at least twenty million dead and immense material devastation. But it won, and in April 1945 Soviet armies took the Nazi capital of Berlin, a convincing symbol of what the Soviet Union was able to do, under Stalin and under communism. Much more than in 1939, the Soviet Union signified great military power. Perhaps, Soviet sympathizers in the West told themselves, Stalin's frightfulness in the 1930s had a point.

Canadian observers were present in Moscow, in the Canadian embassy, to witness the end of the war. Western diplomats usually had little to do in Moscow but observe, and chat among themselves about what they saw. One of them later recalled the experience. His comments suggest the problems of assessing a secretive society even when, thanks to the war, it was obliged to have reciprocal relations with outsiders. "When you talked to Russians," John McCordick observed, "and even then when we were allies, they were very cautious. They had already been so indoctrinated about talking to foreigners or revealing state secrets and to them practically everything seemed to be a state secret so that it was not easy to get beyond banalities and superficialities...."[6]

It was equally difficult penetrating through the fog of propaganda that had enveloped the Soviet Union since 1917. To quote the same Canadian observer:

> It was a strange amalgam of slogans and teaching, what they'd received in school and university, all with a large Marxist component, and prejudices. And even then—we're going back now to the mid-forties—even then people had lost a lot of their knowledge and contact with the so-called outside world. With the Russians one of the greatest difficulties was to bridge this gap of ignorance and to get around the difficulty in using words which to them had a totally different meaning than to us. "Democracy" is the best example of all.[7]

Such experiences, and they were universal among Westerners stationed in Moscow during the war, suggested that a basis for postwar co-operation would not be easy to find. Co-operation or no, the shape of the postwar world was already becoming apparent. In 1944 the Western allies, including Canadians, landed on the European mainland and advanced into Germany from the west, while the Soviets swept through Eastern Europe and attacked Germany from the east. When the Germans surrendered in May 1945 the Western allies occupied France, Italy, the Low Countries, Denmark, Norway, western Austria and western Germany. The Red Army occupied eastern Germany, Poland, most of Czechoslovakia, Romania and Bulgaria, while local Communist regimes, installed by local guerrilla resistance movements, held sway in Albania and Yugoslavia.

This was approximately the division that would last throughout the Cold War. It was established by conquest and reflected military power. At first the events of 1945 could be rationalized. Such things had happened before. Conquering armies came, plundered, occupied and left for home, sometimes immediately, sometimes after a transitional period.[8] What would make the Cold War unique was that the conquering armies stayed—in Eastern Europe by force, and in Western Europe by invitation.

The Western powers were tired of war. Public opinion demanded that the troops come home, and they did. Canada demobilized almost completely, down to an armed force (army, navy and air) of 40,000 by 1948. The United States and Great Britain did likewise. Taxes

11

went down, war debts were repaid, wartime regulations were eased or scrapped. Some garrison troops—not including Canadians, who had all returned home by the end of 1946—were kept in Germany and Austria, which were divided into "zones" of occupation, British, French, American and Soviet.

Germany was in ruins, thanks to aerial bombardment and territorial conquest, and the Nazi party in eclipse. Beyond suppressing the Nazis and disarming the Germans, there was little agreement among the occupying powers as to what to do next. The Soviet Union apart, Germany was still the largest country in Europe, with potentially the most efficient economy; and until very recently it had had the strongest war machine. The experience of the war was not easily forgotten, neither in the East nor the West. What to do with Germany was a question that would remain at the centre of Western-Soviet relations. Until that question could be answered, there could be no true agreement among the allies of the Second World War.

NOTES

1. V. Zubok and C. Pleshakov, *Inside the Kremlin's Cold War From Stalin to Khrushchev* (Cambridge, Mass: Harvard University Press, 1996), 19.
2. French-speaking Quebec, though important in the domestic background to Canada's foreign policy, did not have a pronounced influence *as such* over such matters as inter-allied solidarity.
3. F.H. Soward, *Canada in World Affairs, From Normandy to Paris, 1944-1946* (Toronto: Oxford University Press, 1950), 78.
4. Quoted in Reg Whitaker and Gary Marcuse, *Cold War Canada: The Making of a National Insecurity State, 1945–1957* (Toronto: University of Toronto Press, 1994), 12.
5. For a slightly different point of view, see Whitaker and Marcuse, *Cold War Canada*, 16, in which the authors suggest that the "working class" at the end of the Second World War displayed some signs of "continuing militancy" in 1945.
6. Interview with John A. McCordick, Ottawa, April 1990.
7. Ibid.
8. The Napoleonic Wars were followed by an allied occupation of France, from 1815 to 1818; the Franco-Prussian War by a German occupation, 1871 to 1875; and the First World War by an allied occupation of the Rhineland, from 1919 to 1930.

Chapter Two

Drawing the Lines, 1945–1949

In August 1945 two American B-29 bombers dropped two bombs of unparalleled power on the Japanese Empire, devastating the cities of Hiroshima and Nagasaki. These were atomic bombs, and their appearance changed the face of warfare. Many, including those who dropped them, concluded that the bombs also changed the balance of force in the world.

The Japanese promptly surrendered, making unnecessary an invasion of the Japanese home islands. The Canadian government was relieved. Canada would have had to contribute troops to a costly war against Japan. That expense, measured in lives and money, was now moot. Most Canadians thought the real war had ended with the surrender of Germany the previous May and their government was in fact developing elaborate plans for a peacetime country. Unlike prewar Canada, the postwar version would have a secure social safety net, including unemployment insurance, old-age pensions and, it was hoped, comprehensive health insurance. There was little time, and certainly no money, for foreign policy on this agenda.

The Gouzenko Factor

Foreign policy intruded anyway. A code clerk from the Soviet embassy, Igor Gouzenko, chose the first weekend of September 1945 to leave his employ, bringing with him a sheaf of documents that chronicled not one but two Soviet spy rings in Canada. At first Gouzenko found nobody who would listen to him and his heavily accented tale. Finally the Soviet embassy came to the rescue by sending agents to arrest Gouzenko in his apartment, where they broke down the door. Instead of arresting Gouzenko, the Soviets were themselves arrested by the Ottawa police for breaking and entering. Naturally they pleaded diplomatic immunity and were released, but by then Gouzenko and his family had finally been received into Canadian official custody. Their papers were read, their story believed. It was a true story, as it turned out, and very exciting.

The Soviets, it appeared, were extremely interested in the atomic bombs dropped on Japan, as well as a range of other military and industrial information. Canada had been a junior partner in the development of the bomb, and so Canada had attracted Soviet attention.

This dramatic incident, perched as it was on the bridge between war and peace, has often been identified as the starting gun of the Cold War. That it contributed to the worsening of relations between Canada and the Soviet Union, and between the Western powers and the Soviets generally, is beyond question. It was not, however, a signal for instant hostility or even a freeze in relations. Instead, it introduced a series of bothersome questions that, at first, no-one wanted to ask—perhaps fearing what the answers might be. Was the Soviet Union truly an ally? Was the Gouzenko affair an indication of deep Soviet hostility?

The Canadian prime minister, William Lyon Mackenzie King, was one of those who would have preferred not to ask questions. Seventy years old when Gouzenko knocked on Canada's door, eighteen years prime minister, King had not survived as long as he had by confronting great issues head-on. King's first instinct was to send Gouzenko back to the Soviet embassy and not ask about the consequences. When he learned what Gouzenko had brought with him, he was puzzled and somewhat confused about what to do. It would be better, King believed, not to let a great international incident occur in Canada. His country's finely balanced politics might not stand the strain, and anyway there was enough to do confronting Canada's fractious provincial governments, let alone Joseph Stalin.

If there was to be trouble, King seems to have decided, then it had better be important. The best way to certify importance of any international issue was to get Canada's great power allies to take the matter seriously, and so, a few weeks after Gouzenko's appearance, King travelled to Washington, to confer with President Harry Truman.[1] Truman, to King's surprise, did not seem to take the matter very seriously; no more did his acerbic undersecretary of state, Dean Acheson,[2] who instead lectured the Canadian prime minister on the power of the United States. So King travelled on to see Clement Attlee, the British prime minister, in London.

Attlee had troubles of his own, including deteriorating relations with the Soviet Union, which was attempting to exploit differences between Great Britain and the United States. Soviet policy, in British eyes, was true to Marxist-Leninist ideology, which claimed that with the big war over the Western powers would fall to fighting among themselves for scarce markets for their products. Attlee, knowing

14

that Great Britain was economically devastated by the war, could not afford to fight for markets. He was too busy borrowing money from the Americans to fight with them. Because they could not afford it, he and his Labour party government resented all the more Soviet power as displayed in Eastern Europe and Communist meddling in Western Europe. Attlee therefore was neither surprised nor confused by the Gouzenko affair. From the British point of view it was only to be expected. The world, King was told, had changed. In the words of the British Chiefs of Staff to a meeting of Commonwealth prime ministers in April 1946, "Recent developments make it appear that Russia is our most probable potential enemy, far more dangerous than a revived Germany."

What was King's reaction, and what was the reaction of Canadian officials surrounding him?

According to an early history of Canadian postwar foreign relations, they were "in more general agreement with the British than the general public could have realized at this time."[3] This stance was confirmed the following spring, 1946, when Winston Churchill, the former British prime minister, delivered a speech in Fulton, Missouri, with President Truman seated approvingly on the platform behind him. An "iron curtain" had descended across Europe, Churchill declaimed, and behind it lurked a monstrous tyranny. The West must wake up to the fact.

Mackenzie King had been consulted on the speech beforehand, and the Canadian ambassador in Washington, Lester Pearson, had read it and approved. King listened to Churchill on the radio, and immediately phoned his congratulations. Rather to his surprise, he got through, and spent a few minutes telling Churchill and President Truman what he thought.

The Canadian prime minister was a complex man, seldom completely seized of any single course of action or analysis. He saw foreign policy as a bothersome and dangerous chore, apt to interfere with his primary task of keeping a political balance among Canada's regions, languages, and economic interests. He was certainly worried about Gouzenko, but not primarily because he saw Soviet subversion as an immediate threat to Canada's well-being. The Soviet Union was far away, and Canadian Communists were few. Rather, he was concerned about the Soviet Union's reaction to Canada's announcement to the world that a Soviet spy ring had been operating in Canada and the subsequent arrest, conviction and imprisonment of a number of suspects. Perhaps Gouzenko was an isolated incident, hoped King, and not an indication of widespread Soviet spying. More parochially, he also prayed that the Soviets would not blame him, or Canada, because of the adverse worldwide publicity the Soviet Union had received. King liked to be liked, and he liked above all a peaceable image. The first chance he got, at a peace conference in Paris in June 1946, King trailed around a reception hoping to intercept the Soviet foreign minister, Molotov, to convey (and receive) his message of peace. Molotov prudently avoided the encounter. Meanwhile King's undersecretary for external affairs (a title recently changed to deputy foreign minister) equally prudently ordered in a library on espionage so that he might equip himself for the struggles to come.

Did the Soviets blame King for the bad press they received? Not exactly. They knew the charges were true. In a society operated by a fearful and irascible dictator, the first task was always to blame whomever they could catch. On receipt of the news of Gouzenko's defection, the Soviet government established, at the highest level, a special commission to investigate the flaws in Soviet intelligence gathering that had led to this fiasco.[4] Soviet officials were recalled from Canada to meet an uncertain fate. Moscow even issued a grudging public statement that came close to admitting that Gouzenko's charges were true. There was, it seems, no interest in Moscow in provoking a crisis between East and West, and certainly no intention of worsening relations along a fault line dividing capitalist democracies from the Communist world.

The View from the East

Not yet, at any rate. Soviet policy toward the West may have had more to do with the real agenda of Mackenzie King's government—domestic reconstruction and economic security. The Soviet leadership, supported by orthodox Marxist economics, firmly believed the West would quickly face a severe economic crisis. This notion would not have seemed strange even in the West at this time. Many economists and many politicians feared and predicted an economic downturn at the end of the war. That fear was why Mackenzie King put such emphasis on economic reconstruction and social security at the end of the war.

Expectation of, and hope for, an economic depression suggested that the Soviet Union need not hasten events when in the not-so-long run the West would find its resistance undermined by a crisis of over-production. The devastation of the western part of the USSR also suggested a certain prudence, as well as a need for Western aid if, in the fullness of time, such aid could be made available.

These general considerations of Soviet policy present a paradox.

On the one hand, Soviet analysis of the economic situation of the Western powers was radically mistaken. On the other hand, that analysis suggested that a prudent wait-and-see policy would prove fruitful. In the meantime the Soviet Union should do nothing rash to provoke the Western powers.

But these long-range considerations were only half the story. The Soviets in the last year of the war had won mighty victories and conquered much territory from the Balkans to the Baltic Sea. A large Soviet army sat in eastern Germany, keeping the Germans down and extracting German industrial machinery to rebuild war damage back home. The presence of Soviet troops in the centre of Europe was a measure of national security as well as a symbol of Soviet power. In the view of Stalin and his advisers, these were achievements they could not afford to let go. But, as it would turn out, what was short-term power was long-term weakness.

Some of the peoples of Eastern and Central Europe, such as the Czechs, the Serbs and the Bulgarians, were not anti-Russian. Some were, including the peoples of the three Baltic republics, Estonians, Latvians, Lithuanians; the Poles; the Romanians; the Hungarians. In the Baltic States, which were annexed to the Soviet Union as the spoils of the Hitler-Stalin pact of 1939, Stalin could apply force directly. In the other countries, he preferred if possible to work through intermediaries. Local Communists naturally found the presence of the Soviet Red Army a heaven-sent opportunity, and in most places there were enough non-Communists in the political left and centre who were willing to go along.

Initially, the Soviets formed "Popular Front" administrations, coalitions of parties of the centre and left, in which Communists played a key but not exclusive role. Free elections occurred only in Czechoslovakia and to a lesser degree Hungary. Elsewhere fraud and coercion weighed more than votes. But if the appearance of consent and thus the facade of democracy were to be maintained, fraud and coercion were the least the Communists could do. (The contradiction between facade and reality was, of course, a dilemma of Stalin's own creation.)

The Western powers were distressed. They had not fought the war to establish or re-establish undemocratic regimes in Europe or anywhere else. (Inevitably, the Western powers had blind spots: the British-sponsored government in Greece was hardly democratic, and the British and French colonial empires were not models of democracy.) A complicated series of protests and recriminations ensued.

As the war had turned in their favour, the allies had realized that the end of the war would be complicated. They held three-power (British, American and Soviet) summits at Teheran (November 1943), Yalta (February 1945) and Potsdam (August 1945) to iron out anticipated difficulties. Starting in April 1945 there was the United Nations Organization, quickly abbreviated as the UN, which assembled all the countries that had gone to war against Germany in a single world body. The UN's mission was to preserve the peace. And starting in September 1945 there was a four-power (with the addition of France) Council of Foreign Ministers to manage ongoing controversies and prepare for postwar peace treaties.

The Soviet Union was a willing participant in all these bodies. In the case of the United Nations, which was founded at a conference at San Francisco in April 1945, Stalin went out of his way to be agreeable to the Americans on large issues, while his diplomats at the same time established that they could be tough and unyielding over small things. All the great powers wanted to join, but they wanted to join safely, and so each great power—the United States, Great Britain, France, the Soviet Union and China—was given the right to veto UN actions deemed obnoxious to its interests. The UN was founded, it included all the great powers, and it was given a headquarters in the United States itself.

Canadians were not, of course, present at the three-power summits or at the meetings of the Council of Foreign Ministers, although the Canadian government was regularly fed information by the British and to a lesser extent the Americans. Canadians were, however, present at San Francisco and at the regular sessions of the UN that followed, and Canada sent a delegation headed by Prime Minister King to a peace conference held in Paris in the summer of 1946.

Those present at San Francisco and later conferences were surprised and repelled by what they saw of Soviet behaviour and attitudes. According to F.H. Soward, who in 1951 composed a history of the early Cold War based on access to secret documents, "The experience had been an enlightening and depressing one which had given [Canadian delegates] a healthy respect for the calibre of some of the Soviet representatives." Despite misgivings, the Canadians did their best to work with rather than against the Soviets at the Paris Peace Conference. The conference, however, revealed profound divisions between the Western powers and the Soviet Union, while the open forum of the conference and the meetings of the United Nations made the divisions public. Canada's minister of external affairs, Louis St. Laurent (appointed to the post in September 1946), characterized the United Nations as "impotent," no place for Canada to make a positive contribution.[5]

Atomic weaponry quickly became a major area of stalemate between the Soviet Union and the Western world. The Soviet Union deliberately behaved as if the bomb was a negligible commodity, and the Soviet archives have revealed that this was precisely Stalin's policy. The United States would not dare to use the wonder weapon, in the Soviet dictator's view. The Americans might, on the other hand, be tempted to behave as if the bomb gave them a decisive advantage in diplomacy, and the best way to respond to that possibility was to stand firm on matters large and small.[6] In fact in the five years after 1945 the American government never once directly threatened to use the atomic bomb to secure some proximate diplomatic objective. The bomb would not get the Red Army out of Poland, or unseat a Communist dictatorship in Bulgaria. Doubtless it had some other, ultimate use, more proportionate to its unparalleled power. Such possible uses were, of course, Secret.

The Soviet Union may have brushed aside American atomic power as an immediate threat. It did not discount the notion that the bomb conferred power or the possibility that it might eventually be used. Stalin authorized his own bomb project as early as 1943, and kept the American-British-Canadian wartime efforts under surveillance, hence Gouzenko. The Gouzenko affair was a quick and rude introduction to the first arms race after the Second World War. In September 1945 at the latest, the Soviet atomic project received the highest priority.

There has been much discussion in the West about the proposition that sharing of the atomic secret with the Soviet Union might have averted an arms race or, by establishing trust, prevented the Cold War itself. This was certainly part of the motivation of scientists, in Canada, the United States and Great Britain, who conveyed information about the bomb to Moscow through Soviet agents. This notion can now safely be discounted. Stalin saw the bomb as an essential instrument of power politics, and he was determined from the beginning to have it.[7]

Stalin did agree to participate in talks under UN sponsorship to control atomic weaponry. Canada participated enthusiastically in these discussions in 1946 and 1947 through a high-level and very competent delegation, and the discussions received much publicity. The Canadian government, speaking through its reconstruction minister, C.D. Howe, rather casually announced that for its part it would not build a Canadian bomb. This announcement certainly contributed to Canadian self-esteem, but it had no impact on the flow of events internationally.[8] Realistically there was never any chance of atomic control or disarmament. The Americans were not about to

19

surrender the secret of the atomic weapon to the Soviet Union, and from the Soviet point of view there was no need that they do so. Espionage had already taken care of that. Political distrust, not technology, was the key to the atomic arms race.

Relations between the Soviet Union and its former partners grew steadily worse through 1946 and 1947. The main field of contention was defeated Germany, which at the end of the war was divided into four occupation areas, with Britain, France, the Soviet Union and the United States each responsible for one of the zones. Berlin, the former capital of Germany, now located almost 180 kilometres inside the Soviet zone of Germany, was also divided into four occupation zones. Germany presented both a short-term problem and a long-term worry. In the short term, the Germans had to be fed and clothed and heated. This was costly, especially to the British, whose ravaged economy could ill afford the expense. The Americans too found the occupation a burden, and inevitably began to consider how best to make the Germans pay for the costs of their own upkeep. The best way to do this was to shore up the German economy. But somehow this had to be accomplished in a manner consistent with the longer-term worry that with enough encouragement the Germans would again dominate Europe through their superior size, training and organization.

Did it matter what Stalin thought? Was the Soviet Union part of the solution, or part of the problem? News from Moscow was mixed. The Canadian embassy there, isolated from the Soviets since the Gouzenko affair, shared its information and interpretations with the Americans and British. The three produced surprisingly similar conclusions between 1945 and 1947. The Soviet government posed no danger of immediate aggression in Germany, Ottawa was told. The country was too exhausted by the last war to contemplate seriously the next one. The Soviet government was interested above all in its own preservation and that of the privileged class of Communists it had spawned. Left undisturbed, it would not be rash; but if threatened in its privileges and power, it would do anything to preserve them.

The View from Within: Canada's Early Cold War Philosophy

In a lecture in Toronto in January 1947, Louis St. Laurent, Canada's minister of external affairs, sought to define the bases of Canadian foreign policy. St. Laurent was well equipped to do so, even more than the prime minister. The effective leader of the Liberal party in Quebec, St. Laurent enjoyed the respect and support of his native province. He was conscious that he could bridge the gap in under-standing between English and French Canadians, and he believed that foreign policy could be an avenue to mutual understanding rather than a cause of division, as it had been during the conscription crisis in the very recent past.

In his speech, St. Laurent laid down the bases of Canadian foreign policy not just for the immediate future but, as it turned out, for the next fifty years. The speech unequivocally placed Canada in the Western camp in the emerging conflict between the Soviet Union and its erstwhile allies. His speech may thus be seen as the first public definition and justification of Canada's role in the Cold War.

St. Laurent told his Toronto audience five things.

First, with the experience of a divided country during two world wars behind him, he stated that foreign policy must serve Canada's political unity, not destroy it. It should, therefore, engage all Canadians, from whatever background. It could best do this by expressing Canadians' basic values and beliefs.

Second, as a basic value, St. Laurent suggested support for political liberty. Specifically, "a threat to the liberty of Western Europe, where our political ideas were nurtured, was a threat to our way of life."

Third, Canadian foreign policy should sustain the rule of law. Consider, St. Laurent urged his listeners, "the hideous example of the Fascist states [,] of the evil that befalls a nation when the government sets itself above the law." He did not need to add that there was still a country that by its example in Eastern Europe showed it was indifferent to the rule of law.

Fourth, external policy should be based on human values, and moral principles, and not just material considerations.

And fifth, and as a consequence of the fourth principle, Canada must be willing to assume external responsibilities. Given the devastation of Europe, Canada was an island of abundance that had recently sent forth fleets of aircraft and ships, and placed 500,000 soldiers, sailors and aircrew across the Atlantic. Canada had the ability to act, and in St. Laurent's view, and that of the government he represented, that meant it had a duty to act. In the international sphere, St. Laurent identified the nations of the British Common-wealth, France, and the United States as like-minded countries with which Canadians felt a special identity. St. Laurent did not need to mention unfriendly countries or the Soviet Union in particular; its omission from his list of friendly relationships spoke volumes.

A notable feature of St. Laurent's policy was its prescription for relations with Canada's allies. He did not need to stress that French

Canadians in the past had been unhappy about too close or too auto-matic ties to Great Britain. France existed in the speech mainly as a rhetorical flourish, since there was no realistic chance of very close or important bilateral relations. The United States was a different matter. There, connections should be close, but not too close. "The relationship between a great and powerful neighbour and its small-er neighbour at best is far from simple." Canada would do its duty with and in North America, but would not assume that the world's problems could be avoided by withdrawing into regionalism. Canada would couple its positioning in the Cold War with a quest for broad, many-sided relationships, with as many countries of like mind as possible. As a trading nation, Canada depended on external relations, on a friendly environment abroad. These conditions had always defined Canada's strategic position and guaranteed its security.

Finally, St. Laurent's speech was remarkable for a sense of propor-tion. Canada was "a secondary power." It would co-operate in "con-structive international action" but would not waste its breath or try others' patience by preaching a higher form of duty or responsibility that only larger countries could bear. "There is little point," St. Laurent advised his audience, "in a country of our stature recom-mending international action if those who must carry the major bur-den of whatever action is taken are not in sympathy."

For Canada, then, the Cold War was about relations, cool tending to hostile, with the Soviet Union, which threatened Canada's envi-ronment. It was also about relations with the United States, warm tending toward melting. It was the task of Canadian leaders and diplomats to keep them warm without going the extra step into a complete merger of interests and, eventually, countries. This was a difficult task because of the similarities, cultural, economic and even political, between English-speaking Canada (70% of the country) and the United States.

Those similarities between Canadian and American societies were reinforced by the experience of the recently concluded world war. The war had been almost universally supported in English-speaking North America and it remained a positive experience even in retro-spect. Civilian support had been mobilized behind support for the fighting troops. Supplies for the war moved freely back and forth across the border. Priorities in Canada were matched by priorities in the United States. Both countries assembled and dispatched large armies overseas. Demobilized now, they could be reassembled if there was need; the experience of the war showed that such a need could exist and could be justified.

Alongside the memories of the war were the memories of the prewar, of the hesitant approach to confronting Hitler and the other prewar dictators, symbolized by the policy of appeasement. Appeasement, the policy of seeking peace through concessions to an actually or potentially hostile country (thus winning peace and possibly friendship), had become through its failure to halt Hitler a dirty word, a diplomatic taboo.

A million Canadians had direct experience, as military veterans, of the sequel to appeasement between 1939 and 1945. The senior personnel of Canada's diplomatic service had ringside seats, in London or Washington or at the defunct League of Nations in Geneva, at the rush to war in the later 1930s. Then, the Western powers failed to combine in the face of danger, and as a consequence failed to act effectively even while they still held a preponderance of power over Nazi Germany.

The Western countries, or more precisely the English-speaking ones, including Canada, were physically disarmed, but still psychologically mobilized, in the later 1940s. Drawing on prewar hostility to communism, temporarily suppressed or sublimated during the war, they found it easy to apply reports of Soviet espionage or subversion, or the corruption and coercion of Eastern Europe, to their recent experience of the dangers and ultimate horrors of Nazism.

Memories of alliance transformed into anticipations of danger. Public opinion polls charted a steady rise in fears of a new war. In Canada, at war's end, 46% of a public opinion survey told interviewers that Canada could "get along" with the Soviet Union; but 34% thought otherwise.[9] It may seem curious that this was so, at a time when the United States alone had the capacity to build the ultimate weapon, the atomic bomb, that had ended the Second World War. Canadian public opinion was more alarmed than reassured by this fact. If the United States had the bomb today, surely Stalin would have it tomorrow, though when tomorrow would come was a debatable item.

The Marshall Plan

As the war ended and the allies attempted to devise peace treaties and to solve the thorny problem of Germany in a way that was acceptable to all the wartime partners, many in the West concluded that there was no hope of appealing to the Soviets on the basis of shared values, such as "democracy"—the meaning of the word was not shared and could not be communicated. The best the West could hope for would be to contain the Soviet Union.

The best-known expression of this point of view was found in a telegram from George Kennan of the American embassy in Moscow to his government in 1946. Somewhat sanitized, the telegram was published under the pseudonym "X" in the American journal *Foreign Affairs* early in 1947. There was and could be no true harmony between East and West, X told his readers. Instead, the Western powers had better settle in for a siege, tedious and indefinite, and practise saying "no" to the Soviets. X did not preach urgent action, but rather determination and endurance in the face of an incompatible society that would take advantage of every Western weakness. The Soviet Union must be contained, kept where it was. This policy was "containment," the doctrine of the deep freeze.

Early in 1947 the Council of Foreign Ministers met, interminably, in Moscow. They again surveyed the German problem and again came to no decision. The three Western foreign ministers, with time on their hands, turned to discussing their own concerns. Western Europe had not recovered from the war, a matter of great concern to the British foreign minister, Ernest Bevin, and his French counterpart, Georges Bidault. The American secretary of state, George Marshall, listened carefully, and concluded that something would have to be done. If something were not done, the possibility existed that the demoralized Western Europeans would slide into chaos and possibly Communist control through subversion rather than invasion. The United States would then be dangerously isolated in the world.

The something Marshall had in mind was given form in discussions inside the American government in the spring of 1947, and was announced in June. The United States government would make many billions of dollars available to European governments for the purpose of economic rehabilitation. The Europeans were invited to discuss among themselves how best to manage such a donation. The invitation was extended to all European governments, including the Soviet Union's.

In fact, the economies of Eastern Europe were in far worse shape than those of the West. Several Eastern European governments, though led by Communists, were strongly attracted by the idea of American aid. The Soviet Union, too, was tempted. In its interpretation of events, the offer of billions of dollars in American aid was the result of capitalist weakness. Stalin's government believed that the Americans had no choice but to dole out aid in order to maintain a market for over-production at home. Consequently, the American offer could be manipulated to Soviet advantage, without the Soviet Union having to accept bothersome controls or strings on how the aid money would be spent. Accordingly, the Soviet Union and its East European followers accepted an invitation to a preliminary conference in Paris in June 1947.

The conference, however, took a different turn from that expected by the Soviets. The Western Europeans understood that the offered American aid was an opportunity for co-operation, a chance to establish an international plan with shared criteria and controls. For the Soviet Union, with its hermetically sealed economy and strictly controlled society, this approach was completely unacceptable—as the Americans knew it would be. The Soviet Union abruptly pulled out of the Paris conference, and after a certain hesitation announced it would come no more. The Eastern Europeans were instructed accordingly, and obeyed the orders from Moscow. The lines were now drawn in Europe more obviously than they had been by Churchill's "Iron Curtain" speech the previous year.

The "Marshall Plan," as the American scheme was dubbed, quickly gave rise to a multi-national European Recovery Plan, headquartered in Paris, and dispensing 13.2 billion American dollars. And, to anticipate, the Plan accomplished its purpose, reinforcing Western European morale and creating a political alternative to the temptations of power and brutality on the other side of the Iron Curtain.

The Canadian chargé d'affaires in Moscow, John Holmes, suggested a domestic corollary to the high politics of the Marshall Plan. Many years later he reflected,

> The Politburo probably did not dare accept Marshall Plan aid, which would not only interfere with true socialist reconstruction but also subvert the contempt which citizens must feel for the Western world if they were to believe in their own.... I recall how Ivan Fedorovich, our humble [janitor], regarded a glossy toilet seat we had ordered from the Hudson's Bay Company and exclaimed with awe, after he had installed it, what might be roughly translated as, "That's Canada for you."[10]

Politics, Economics and Foreign Policy

In the face of the X article, the Marshall Plan, and the possibility that the United States might now be ready to take a much more assertive political and economic role in Europe, the Canadian government was debating what position it should take in its foreign policy. The X article had had a profound effect in Ottawa, where all senior diplomats were asked to give their reactions. Escott Reid, assistant undersecretary, and the external affairs department's "ideas man," urged that

25

the time had come to formalize what had already become a tacit alliance. A direct attack from the Soviet Union, "a Soviet-American war," was unlikely in the near or medium future. Instead, there would be a nibbling away and a softening up, culminating in the encirclement of North America. Such a process, calculated and controllable, favoured the Soviets because it diminished the chance of a war in which the odds were definitely against the USSR. The West did not know how to respond to measures short of war, for which it was difficult to mobilize public opinion, and might even permit the Russians to distance themselves and possibly disavow proxy attacks through one or another of their "satellites."

The West must keep calm. Western policy must act to shore up the economies of Western Europe, as the Marshall Plan proposed. Without saying so, Reid drew on the lessons of appeasement in the 1930s. Public opinion, including liberal or left opinion, would be crucial in securing a unanimous, effective reaction to the projection of Soviet power. The Soviet Union must be fairly treated—a stretch in the conditions of 1947, but a useful prescription nevertheless. There must be "firmness" without "rudeness."

There must be strength, and therefore unity among the Western powers. That meant following, to a very considerable extent, the American lead. "In the event of war," Reid observed, "we shall have no freedom of action in any matter which the United States considers essential." That was not quite the case in time of peace, but Canadian freedom even then would be "limited." In case of conflict or disagreement between the Canadian and American governments, it was entirely possible that some Canadians would take the American point of view, and some Americans, whether they knew it or not, the Canadian. The "similarities" between the two peoples would make this so—in effect, Canadian foreign policy where it touched upon the United States would never be entirely "foreign;" and vice-versa.[11]

Reid's analysis was now sent out for comment within the Department of External Affairs. Reaction flowed in throughout the fall of 1947. Some was positive, some negative, some merely silly. The decline of Britain was noted, and regretted. The farther east the Canadian reader, the more pessimistic. Communism was a dynamic, restless force, according to the Canadian envoy in Prague; uncontrollable and unpredictable, it would seek to expand wherever it could. The United States, which Reid had placed in a kind of balance with the Soviet Union, was in reality a much more benign force in international affairs. Where Canada was concerned, the United States was much more likely to rely on "friendly discussion" rather than "insistence," which, given Canadian public opinion, would be counter-productive.[12] From Moscow, the chargé d'affaires, R.A.D. Ford, saw no grounds for optimism. "At the present time the Soviet system does not seem to give any indication of either mellowing or collapsing. So far as one can see, Stalin is at the peak of his power," but even if Stalin were to die there was no great reason to expect an improvement in Soviet conduct—"wishful thinking."[13]

That, and much more, was the political side of Canadian foreign policy. There was also an economic side, which in 1947 had concerns equally grave. Canada faced a foreign exchange crisis. Briefly, Canadians were spending too much abroad, in trade and aid, and not bringing in enough through exports or imports of capital. This imbalance threatened Canada's ability to buy supplies, ranging from oranges to iron ore, from the United States. Canada's economy would grind to a halt, something the United States government could not afford. Both governments were acting in the uncertain context of the early Cold War. Would Western Europe succumb to communism? Would the two democracies of North America be isolated in a hostile world? No one could tell, and that uncertainty gave a certain edge to the events that followed.

In the fall of 1947, the Canadian government undertook exploratory talks with the United States government on the possibility of a customs union, which would create a tariff-free common market between the two countries. The talks progressed, by the spring of 1948, to the point where a clear political decision was needed—to proceed or to cancel. Mackenzie King, still prime minister, made the decision to stop and draw back. Canada, he sensed, would not survive such a profound integration into the American economy, and American assistance through a free trade treaty, however well meant, would overwhelm a country one-tenth the size of the United States.

King saw an alternative to a customs union in the Marshall Plan, which permitted Europeans to use American funds from the Plan to purchase goods from other "offshore" countries—meaning, among others, Canada. By applying the American dollars received from such purchases to Canadian cash shortages, Canada was able to use the Marshall Plan to help solve its balance-of-payments problem.

The Americans for their part were prepared to wait on events. Canada's emergency trade measures making use of the Marshall Plan in the fall of 1947 worked for the time being. The Truman administration faced a presidential election in the fall of 1948, which it stood

27

a good chance of losing. A customs union with Canada could only be sold to the American electorate, especially in states with products competitive with Canada's, at a time of grave external crisis—a retreat to "Fortress North America," for example—or after a prolonged preparation of the American electorate for the achievement of a foreign policy goal that had existed "since the foundation of the Republic."

More broadly, Canada in the 1945-9 period concentrated its foreign policy energies on Western Europe and the United States. The Canadian government was aware of a larger world beyond the North Atlantic, but considered that world less important, less crucial, than the traditional Canadian linkages with Europe and the United States. Few Canadians came from China or Japan or India. The Chinese civil war, reaching its climax in 1949 with the victory of Mao Zedong and his Communists, was exciting but, on the whole, remote. Paradoxically, China was considered too vast for any Western—and certainly any Canadian—intervention to do any good. Canadian trade with the Far East was minimal and Canadian interests proportionately small. There were no serious democratic forces in China as there were in Western Europe: historically, ideologically and economically Canada counted itself out in East Asia.[14] Canada's national interest, as the government conceived it, was limited by circumstance—Canada's established patterns of immigration and trade—and by necessity. Canadian resources were not infinite, nor, in the government's cautious assessment, were those of the West in general.

NATO

In February 1948 the coalition Popular Front government of Czechoslovakia came unglued. Fed up with Communist subversion of the country's democratic institutions, ministers from the democratic parties resigned, thereby depriving the government of its majority in parliament. Public opinion polls predicted that in any election the Communists would lose heavily, and the democrats hoped to achieve just that.

Unfortunately, they reckoned without the determination of the Communist prime minister, and the weakness of the democratic Czech president. The Communists immediately brought armed workers into the streets of Prague, intimidated the president, and appointed a government much more strongly Communist than the one it replaced. The Czech foreign minister, Jan Masaryk, a prominent democrat, briefly joined this new government while apparently making preparations to flee to Paris. But Masaryk was murdered by the Communists, thrown out of his apartment window, at the beginning of March.

Mackenzie King, who knew and liked Masaryk, was moved. He was moved even more by an urgent telegram from the British government, proposing secret discussions among the three North Atlantic English-speaking powers—Canada, the United States and Great Britain. These discussions took place in Washington later in March, under conditions of the strictest security. Only a few members of the Canadian government, and the American and the British, knew what was going on. Stalin also knew, because one of the members of the British delegation was a senior Soviet spy.

These tripartite March talks came to the conclusion that a more formal link among the Western nations might now be necessary. A larger discussion should be held, bringing in the Belgians, Dutch, Luxembourgers, and French, with an eye to establishing a formal alliance between the nations of Western Europe and the two North American democracies.

Canada had a number of objectives in these discussions. The first was security, which Lester Pearson, the leader of the Canadian delegation, described as requiring "an overwhelming preponderance of force." To achieve this goal meant linking nations. It also meant, Pearson argued, appealing to forces within nations: attracting the "apathetic, fearful or doubtful" to the Western cause. (This was a revealing reference to the fact that NATO was about internal security as much as or more than external aggression; but the Canadians did not succeed in importing direct references to internal security into the North Atlantic Treaty.)[15] These requirements, to Pearson's mind, implied the establishment of an alliance that would commit the United States to the common defence of the West. That was only the first step. The Canadians preferred a multilateral grouping of equals, in which all member states would be committed to the defence of one another. And, with an eye to the "apathetic, fearful or doubtful," such an alliance must appeal to positive political ideals.

Pearson also wanted an alliance that would include political, economic and cultural goals. His prime minister, Mackenzie King, wanted some reference to economic co-operation that would justify, retrospectively, his refusal to go along with an American customs union. Some of Pearson's colleagues, especially the waspish Canadian ambassador to Washington, Hume Wrong, were doubtful about including an economic and cultural plank. The Europeans, who wanted an uncomplicated security guarantee from the United States, were similarly reluctant. The British were lukewarm, and only a few American officials saw merit in a larger alliance. They knew, however, that Congress, jealous of American sovereignty, would not see much of an advantage in encumbering American freedom of action any more than was strictly necessary.

The second round of Washington talks lasted into the fall of 1948. They coincided with a Soviet attempt to squeeze the Western allies out of their occupation sectors in the isolated city of Berlin by not allowing Western vehicles carrying the supplies needed to maintain West Berlin and its people to travel across the long road through the Soviet zone of Germany to the city. The British and Americans, but conspicuously not the Canadians, met the crisis by airlifting supplies into the beleaguered city for almost a year. The Canadian government viewed the Berlin episode as a post-colonial rather than a pre-Cold War experience. Deciding that Canadian participation was being taken for granted by its larger partners, especially the British, who in his opinion were treating Canada like a colony, Mackenzie King balked and refused to mobilize aircraft or aircrew for the enterprise. War did not come over Berlin, but during 1949-50 tensions were very high. The tensions stimulated agreement over a North Atlantic security treaty, and helped overcome misgivings among negotiators.

It was no surprise when the Washington conferees produced an agreed-upon draft that a third, expanded, set of discussions would be needed in early in 1949 to convert into the draft agreement into a treaty. By then President Truman had been triumphantly re-elected and had appointed a new secretary of state, Dean Acheson. It was left to Acheson to bring the draft North Atlantic Treaty to fruition.

Acheson had to negotiate on two fronts. He had to manage a treaty satisfactory to all the United States' potential allies, now eleven in number. He had also to navigate the treaty through ratification by the United States Senate. Acheson had a low opinion of Congress and a high opinion of its potential for mischief. He knew that some Senators would be allergic to any proposals that might limit American sovereignty. Yet the Canadians were holding out for an article in the treaty that would promote economic and cultural co-operation.

Wrong was instructed by Pearson, who had entered politics and was now external affairs minister in a government headed by Louis St. Laurent, to inform the Americans that failure to secure a cultural and economic article would damage the treaty's chances in Canada. This was a very questionable argument, but it is a formula often used by states to signify the fact that they put great importance on a given demand. Acheson, sick at home with the flu, was visited by the Canadian ambassador and two senior State Department officials, both of whom favoured what the Canadians wanted. A compromise was struck. An article on non-military co-operation was included—Article Two of the North Atlantic Treaty. But the article was so vaguely formulated that it did not compel the member states of the alliance to do anything. Acheson expected it to be a dead letter, and so it was. The North Atlantic Treaty was signed by the allies, including Canada, in April 1949 in Washington. It then sailed triumphantly past the Senate.

It is useful to pause and ask what the North Atlantic Treaty said and what it did. It linked eleven nations of Western Europe and North America in a security alliance. It was an alliance of equals, and not just a guarantee by the most powerful, the United States, that it would defend the rest. An attack on one would be considered to be an attack on all. The alliance would involve the threat or promise of military force, although initially it had no military apparatus, no General Staff, no headquarters and no army. These things were not mentioned in the treaty. There would be a North Atlantic council on which all members were represented.

Were the member-states equally represented? In theory, yes. But was not the United States much more equal than others? Was it not richer and more powerful and therefore predominant? It is possible to see NATO as a projection of American power and the allies, including Canada, as willing satellites of the United States. But that would be to misread the history of NATO. The alliance proved to be an effective instrument for many of the smaller powers and the allies were by no means bereft of influence. That was precisely because NATO was useful to the United States, but also because the Americans were unable, and in any case did not want, to micro-manage the affairs of their allies.[16] Symbolically, NATO demonstrated to Americans, voting Americans, that the United States was not alone in the world, as a country or as a democracy. That made it attractive to American politicians. NATO also created a network of obligations, and the Americans had no difficulty in understanding that the obligations were reciprocal. The allies required care and feeding, sometimes as little as possible, but care and feeding nevertheless. Strong and willing allies were, from the American point of view, much to be preferred to weak and dependent ones. The loss of even one democratic (or potentially democratic) country, after Czechoslovakia, was to be avoided at all costs.

This attitude was evident in the American desire to prop up Canada in 1947-8, at the time of the abortive customs union negotiations. It was apparent in American economic aid to Europe, before and after the Marshall Plan. It was apparent, then and later, in

American encouragement of European economic and political co-operation.

Where did Canada fit in this larger American scheme of co-operation and alliance? Baldly, the more desperate the situation, the more important Canada was. In 1947-8, when the prospects for Europe looked darkest, Canada bulked larger in American thoughts; and the same was true in reverse. A Fortress North America, isolated in a totalitarian world, would have been a united North America, in fact if not in name. Under the circumstances, form would eventually have followed substance, as the common emergency overcame the constitutional scruples of both parties. The successful launching of the Marshall Plan, coupled with the establishment of NATO, removed some of the urgency in Canadian-American relations. Both countries were relieved: the Canadians because Canadian sovereignty would have been threatened if not submerged in an unavoidably close bilateral relationship; and the Americans because they had secured bigger and more important allies than the Canadians.

The NATO negotiations testify to the limits of Canada's effective foreign policy. Throughout the NATO talks, the Canadian government did its best to limit the future alliance to democracies, and to the North Atlantic area. It did not prevail. The United States wanted, and probably needed, the co-operation of Portugal, a dictatorship, in order to secure island bases in the Atlantic. The French insisted on the inclusion of Algeria, effectively a colony and in any case outside the North Atlantic region. Because France was crucial to the coherence and credibility of the alliance, it got its way. And the Western Europeans and the Americans found it desirable to bolster Italy, whose government in 1948 faced a major challenge from domestic Communists.

The North Atlantic Treaty Organization, NATO, proved to be one of the longest-lasting alliances ever created. Originally more of a political creation than a military one, it soon acquired a military arm that, over time, became its most important feature. A General Staff, a headquarters, a supreme commander, and an army all came into existence. All this conformed to Acheson's conception of the alliance, and it proved to have more staying power than Pearson originally imagined.

Was the Canadian quest for Article 2 misconceived? Was it an example of misplaced Canadian idealism? Acheson certainly saw it that way, and said so. NATO was only politically possible if it interfered as little as possible with the important domestic interests of its partners. In its origins, and as it developed, it did not do so.

Admittedly this emphasis left little room for consultation or agreement on other matters. Such matters included non-European security, American adventures in the Third World, fuel shortages in the 1970s and 1980s. Though NATO occasionally "conferred" on such subjects, it had no mechanism for reaching or enforcing agreement. The Western allies therefore found themselves from time to time pursuing widely divergent policies. Happily, and possibly accidentally, the alliance never fell apart under these pressures; but perhaps that was because, for much of its existence, NATO was marginal to the main interests of its partners.

NOTES

1. Harry Truman, a Democrat, was elected vice-president of the United States on a ticket with President Franklin D. Roosevelt in 1944. On Roosevelt's death in April 1945, Truman became president.
2. Acheson's parents were both Canadians and his father had served in the army during the Riel Rebellion of 1885. Acheson thought he had a perfect right to be censorious where Canadians were concerned.
3. F.H. Soward, "A Survey of Canadian External Policy," chapter one, "Canada's Position in 1946," mimeograph, 12, John Holmes Papers, Canadian Institute of International Affairs.
4. V. Zubok and C. Pleshakov, *Inside the Kremlin's Cold War* (Cambridge, MA: Harvard University Press, 1996), 146.
5. Quoted in Soward, "A Survey of Canadian External Policy," chapter one, 15.
6. David Holloway, *Stalin and the Bomb* (New Haven: Yale University Press, 1994), 164-6.
7. Ibid., 132-3.
8. Howe made the remark off the cuff; the issue had not been discussed in Cabinet. Nevertheless, it represented a consensus view in the Canadian government, which was reinforced by the understanding that a bomb project was simply too costly—estimated at 20% of GNP—for Canada to undertake.
9. Quoted in Reg Whitaker and Gary Marcuse, *Cold War Canada: The Making of a National Insecurity State, 1945-1957* (Toronto: University of Toronto Press, 1994), 12.
10. John Holmes, "Moscow 1947-1948: Reflections on the Origins of My Cold War," in L. Black and N. Hillmer, eds., *Nearly Neighbours: Canada and the Soviet Union from Cold War to Détente and Beyond* (Kingston, ON: Ronald Frye, 1988), 46.
11. Reid, "The United States and the Soviet Union: A Study of the

Possibility of War and Some of the Implications for Canadian Policy," 30 August 1947, *Documents on Canadian External Relations, 1947* (Ottawa: Department of External Affairs and International Trade, 1993) 367-82; henceforth referred to as *DCER*.

12. R.M. Macdonnell to Pearson, 25 September 1947, *DCER*, 13, 387-9.

13. Ford to Pearson, 10 October 1947, *DCER*, 13, 395-6.

14. See Paul M. Evans and B. Michael Frolic, eds. *Reluctant Adversaries: Canada and the People's Republic of China, 1949-1970* (Toronto: University of Toronto Press, 1991), especially chapters one and two.

15. Pearson, "Proposed Pact of Mutual Assistance," quoted in James Eayrs, *In Defence of Canada,* 4 (Toronto: University of Toronto Press, 1980), 69.

16. There were exceptions, inevitably. In the best known instance, American interest in the 1948 Italian election was intense, and spilled over into aid to friendly parties. The Americans subsidized and pressured and cajoled and propagandized, in Italy and elsewhere, though not, in this period, in Canada. But the exceptions do not disprove the rule, as Alan Milward and others have shown: see Alan Milward, *The Reconstruction of Western Europe* (Berkeley: University of California Press, 1984), or Geir Lundestad, "Empire by Invitation?" The United States and Western Europe, 1945-1952," *Journal of Peace Research,* 23 (1986), 263-77.

Chapter Three

Excursions and Alarms, 1950–1957

The Korean War

The 1950s began with a bang. On Sunday, June 25, 1950, the army of North Korea, a Communist state, invaded South Korea, its non-Communist neighbour. The war that resulted lasted for three years and consumed 2,000,000 lives. About 480,000 American troops, and 10,600 Canadian troops travelled to Korea; of the Canadians 406 never returned. The war brought East and West into armed confrontation, and militarized the Western alliance. If the events of the late 1940s determined that there would be a Cold War, the Korean War determined what form it would take.

The two Koreas were creations of the Second World War. In 1945, when the Japanese surrendered, the Americans had occupied the Korean peninsula south of the 38th parallel, while the Soviets accepted the Japanese surrender north of that line. The two occupying powers then installed governments they considered appropriate in their respective zones.

Korea was a small item on the American agenda. It paled by comparison with relations with defeated Japan, where the United States was the sole occupying partner and dominant power after 1945. It certainly paled by comparison with the civil war between Communists and non-Communists in China, where armies a million strong contended for supremacy over the world's most populous nation.

The Americans had demobilized after 1945, and by 1947 were desperately short of troops. The conclusion seemed obvious. Needing troops elsewhere, in Japan, in Europe, anywhere, the Americans decided to cut their losses in Korea. They used the United Nations to bless a successor government in South Korea,[1] and in conjunction with the Soviets withdrew from the peninsula in 1949. At the same time the Communists won the Chinese civil war, giving North Korea two friendly land neighbours: the Soviet Union itself, under Stalin, and China with a new government under Mao Zedong.

The United States was not quite sure what to make of the developments in China. Some argued that the Americans should wait and see what the Chinese might do; others judged the Chinese Communists by their own words to be utterly and unchangeably hostile to the United States. Probably as important for American policy was the explosion in September 1949 of a Soviet atomic bomb, ending the American nuclear weapons monopoly. The combination of the so-called "fall of China" and the Soviet breakthrough in nuclear weapons stimulated serious reconsideration of American foreign policy. In the spring of 1950 this reconsideration was embodied in a paper produced for the American National Security Council, known in short form as NSC-68. NSC-68 called for nothing short of mobilization of American will and resources in the face of a soon-to-be overwhelming Communist threat.

As soon as the North Korean invasion occurred, President Syngman Rhee of South Korea appealed for American aid. President Harry Truman and his advisers, including Secretary of State Dean Acheson, concluded that American credibility, the willingness of other countries to believe the promises of the United States government, was at stake. Failure to resist aggression in South Korea would imply a failure to resist aggression in some other, admittedly more important area, such as Western Europe. And there was no doubt that the North Korean action was aggression and not some doubtful border infiltration. The situation, so it seemed to Truman and his advisers, was like Europe in the later 1930s—just over ten years before. At that time the democracies had not resisted fascist aggression until it was too late. Korea thus became a case study in applying the lessons of appeasement. And where the old League of Nations had failed, the new United Nations must succeed.

One consequence of Chinese Communist hostility, as well as the fact that the rival Nationalist Chinese were still holding out on the large island of Taiwan, separated by a wide strait from the mainland, was that the Chinese seat at the United Nations was still occupied by the previous non-Communist Chinese government. The Soviet Union protested this state of affairs, and to signal its discontent boycotted the organs of the United Nations, including the important Security Council. It was, therefore, not present to veto the United Nations' decision to send troops to defend South Korea.

The Canadian government was surprised that the United States should choose to resist in Korea, but was delighted that Truman had chosen the United Nations to be the instrument to resist aggression. But even at the beginning there were divergences between Lester Pearson's reaction and that of Dean Acheson—who was, incidentally, an old friend of many years standing. Acheson was prepared to see intervention in Korea as a test of the United Nations system, but he also saw the North Korean invasion as a heaven-sent opportunity to mobilize the United States and its allies into new international configurations that could resist the spread of communism—NSC-68, in short.

Canadian public opinion was at first hesitant, but as the summer of 1950 drew on and the United States forces under the umbrella of the United Nations suffered some initial defeats, pressure grew on the Canadian government to do something. External Affairs Minister Pearson urged his colleagues to send troops, and at the beginning of August the Cabinet agreed.

The decision to send Canadian troops was a reversal of government policy in two senses. First, the Liberal government was still very sensitive to the issue of national unity. Overseas military commitments occurred only in time of war, and war in the past had meant conscription and serious internal divisions. Second, the Liberals' entire government strategy was based on encouraging employment and social security at home. This strategy might mean, and it had meant, some kinds of foreign aid, ultimately with the idea of stimulating Canadian markets or protecting those that were already there. And it did not preclude an active political foreign policy. Until 1950, however, no one had contemplated the possibility that Canada's international activities, at the UN or in NATO, would mean substantial defence expenditures.

Canadian troops sailed for Korea in 1950 and entered large-scale action as part of a British Commonwealth division in 1951. By then the war had expanded through Chinese intervention in November 1950. After a period of uncertainty the war stabilized very roughly where it began, along the 38th parallel. Although the Korean War is usually thought of as a land war, it was really air power that determined the outcome of the conflict. The United States and its allies, including a small Canadian contingent of pilots, controlled the air. While the ground war kept American and Canadian soldiers apart—and maintained old military patterns that dated back to the First World War or even earlier—the air war brought Canadian and American airmen much closer together. Henceforth Canada's armed forces were closer to American attitudes and accepted US views of the world more readily—though not invariably.

The war ended in stalemate in July 1953. An armistice was signed, bringing an end to the war but not resolving the deep hostility between North and South Korea. The war reinforced South Korea's previously unstable government and determined that that country would follow a capitalist road, eventually to a booming economy and great prosperity. North Korea, governed by a hereditary Communist dictatorship, remained economically retarded, and close to starvation, well into the late 1990s.

One feature of Canada's Korean War effort deserves to be noted. In previous wars the proportion of French Canadians in the armed forces was less than their proportion of the population. That was not the case in Korea. Of the 10,600 Canadians who served in Korea, 3,100 came from Quebec. Despite early fears among politicians in Ottawa, the Korean War was not an occasion for national disunity.

There were certainly misgivings among Canadian diplomats about American military leadership during the war. Lester Pearson was alarmed at the US (and UN) commander General Douglas MacArthur's warlike statements, and even after MacArthur was dismissed by President Truman in April 1951, Canadians remained concerned by what they conceived to be excessive American rigidity. That same month—indeed within days of MacArthur's firing—Pearson made a public speech on Canadian-American relations that expressed some of his reservations.

"The days of relatively easy and automatic political relations with our neighbour are, I think, over," Pearson told a Toronto audience. If Canada needed to criticize the United States, even in public, it would be done. As Pearson also pointed out, the United States was securely engaged in international affairs by the early 1950s: Canada did not have to worry *"whether* the United States will discharge her international responsibilities, but how she will do it and whether the rest of us will be involved."[2] The speech received wide and generally unfavourable coverage in the United States. Luckily for Pearson it was quickly buried by the much greater news of General MacArthur's firing by President Truman.

Pearson's misgivings eventually landed him in hot water with his old friend Acheson; but in the first months of the Korean War they agreed more often than not. Pearson understood that Acheson faced complicated political problems in the United States, and sympathized with his efforts to fend off an increasingly vocal American right wing that wanted an American policy that took a very narrow view of American interests, and that deeply mistrusted foreign entanglements. Yet at bottom Pearson did not like Acheson's concentration of effort on Asia. Pearson was and remained Europe-centred, and Europe is certainly where he thought the main antagonist resided. He was also affected by the growing belief that war, in 1950-1, was becoming more rather than less likely. That danger underlined the necessity for Western prudence in his mind. His belief did not mean that he did not support or sustain the alliances of the Cold War, merely that he and his colleagues in the St. Laurent Cabinet gave the Cold War a slightly different interpretation and practice than did the Americans.

The difference of emphasis can be seen in a discussion between Canadian and American diplomats over atomic weapons and their possible use in June 1951. "The US would, in all probability, regard open and substantial [Soviet] intervention in the Korean War or against Japan as grounds for launching the atomic bomb," Pearson's deputy minister, A.D.P. Heeney, wrote. "They might decide to launch an attack at once on Moscow. If they could be induced to accept an obligation to notify us in advance before a strike from Canadian bases, we might have a final opportunity to make our views known."[3]

The Canadians wanted to make their views known because they had less and less confidence in American judgement of the international scene. "The impression was growing in Canada," Pearson told Acheson in June 1951, "not so much as the result of official statements by members of the United States Administration as for other reasons, that opinion in the United States was hardening in the direction of the inevitability of war with the Soviet Union." Acheson, "rather surprisingly," agreed that close observers of the American media "had every reason for that impression." But, the secretary of state urged, the Canadians should "trust in the good sense of the American people." Meanwhile, they should let Acheson carry on the struggle against "the powers of darkness in his own country."[4]

Canadians had no choice but to trust the Americans, and no chance, as they now realized, at last-minute consultation in the event of war. The effect was to push Canadian diplomacy back, away from the brink of war, where Canada's voice would not be heard, toward the prevention of war. Pearson through the rest of 1951 and 1952 consistently—and sometimes unrealistically—sought out every avenue for conciliation and compromise between the United Nations and the Communists in Korea, where a military stalemate now existed and cease-fire negotiations were beginning. Acheson eventually became greatly exercised, and in November 1952 even took his arguments for a firmer Western posture against the Communists to Ottawa for a meeting with the Canadian Cabinet. He found sympathy, but no willingness to undercut Pearson's diplomacy. In any case, Acheson's party, the Democrats, had been defeated in the recent presidential elections, and however vigorously he quacked, he was a lame duck.

The Nuclear Factor

Acheson did, however, find Canada an ally that was willing to shoulder its share of the general Western defence burden. In the early 1950s

Defence Minister Brooke Claxton presided over the greatest peacetime build-up of Canada's armed forces, from a strength of 40,000 in 1950 to 120,000 a few years later. The military budget expanded proportionately, while Claxton's colleague C.D. Howe was put in charge of spending $5 billion on rearmament. Because the Canadian economy was expanding, and living standards were rising, the country took the immediate rearmament effort more or less in stride.

Korea was the occasion, but it was not the main cause or object of Canada's expanded defence effort. The same was true of the United States, and of the other NATO allies. With the testing of an atomic bomb by the Soviet Union in 1949 and as tensions continued to grow between the Soviet Union and the West, NATO member-states took steps to establish a military arm. A Supreme Allied Commander, Europe, was appointed: American General Dwight D. Eisenhower, who had commanded the invasion of northwest Europe in 1944. His headquarters, labelled SHAPE, Supreme Headquarters, Allied Powers Europe, were just outside Paris.

With its military arm established, NATO looked for troops to fill it. Canada contributed a brigade group, which was expandable into a much larger military force in time of crisis. This brigade group was stationed with the British Army of the Rhine, the British force in Germany, and remained with the British until 1968. Canada also sent an air division of twelve interceptor squadrons, and in the Atlantic assigned ships to NATO anti-submarine patrols.

NATO's main task was to try to match the superior land forces of the Soviet Union and its Eastern European satellites. A conference in Lisbon in 1952 set troop targets for each of the member-states, and in doing so set the stage for continuing disappointment and unfulfilled expectations. There were two principal expectations when the NATO military structure was established: first, that NATO would establish a military force to which the Europeans would contribute the larger part; and second, that the American and Canadian troops who were sent to Europe in 1951 would not be there effectively forever.

Yet American troops are still, in the late 1990s, in Europe, and Canada's NATO forces remained right up to the end of the Cold War. The American and Canadian troops remained only in part because the Soviet threat persisted. In larger part they remained because the NATO structure established in 1951 was so finely balanced that it seemed dangerous to upset it—the old argument that the stability of Europe required and indeed demanded North American and especially American participation.

NATO was a large part of Canada's self-image in the 1950s, an image not of a peacekeeper, but of a staunch ally doing its bit, main-

taining its self-respect, and deserving to be treated with consideration. Despite disappointments in overall military contributions, the
NATO army of the 1950s was not as weak as is often supposed, and
the Canadian reinforced brigade was well equipped, well motivated
and well led. The air division was well equipped with the latest aircraft, and Canada's contribution at sea included an aircraft carrier
and fourteen destroyers.

Strategy in the foreign affairs of most NATO members in the
1950s was dominated by the atomic bomb. At first the preoccupation
was with the size and type of bomb, which caused ferocious debates
inside the American government in 1950-1. By the mid-1950s the
Americans and the Soviets had developed more powerful weapons,
the hydrogen or thermonuclear bombs, and were busy perfecting
them in seemingly endless tests, while studying their effect on sim-
ulations of civilian and military targets. Sometimes the targets were
not simulated. In one notorious case, the Soviets exploded an atomic
device high above some of their own troops, to discover what might
occur. And in North America tests were televised so that Americans,
and Canadians too, could see what would happen in case of a nuclear
attack. Meanwhile airborne fallout from nuclear tests blew across
North America. While governments vigorously denied that the fallout posed a serious health hazard, by the mid-1950s the media and
consequently the public were giving the matter uneasy attention.
Annihilation, it seemed, might come in one sudden, blinding burst,
or as slow poison from atomic tests. Newspapers published maps
showing how their particular locality would be affected by an atomic explosion, while governments busied themselves with civil
defence. Some private citizens built bomb shelters and hotels in the
United States, frequently visited by Canadians, placed maps on each
floor indicating where their guests should go in case of nuclear
attack. What was the most important fact about the new half century, *Chatelaine* magazine asked itself. "The argument stopped by
sudden consent, for we all recognized what it was! the Atom Bomb."[5]

The fear of atomic weapons and nuclear war was heightened
in May 1955 when eight of the Communist nations of Eastern
Europe signed the Warsaw Pact treaty, bringing their armed forces
under a unified military command. The West's and NATO's perception of the Soviet bloc as a strong, unified—and inimical—force was
reinforced.

Atomic weapons had one great advantage. After the initial investment in production facilities, they were cheap. However, Canada
itself did not want to devote billions of dollars for its own bomb production facilities. Throughout this period Canada relied on the

41

American nuclear stockpile for defence, and until 1959 sold the United States almost every tonne of uranium produced in this country's burgeoning uranium mining industry—$331 million worth in 1959, of which $311 million was exported, making it Canada's leading mineral export that year, and placing it just behind lumber and timber among Canada's principal exports. The Americans, at least until the late 1950s, believed that they needed the uranium.

The United States developed in the 1950s a vast stockpile of nuclear weapons, and fielded 600 B-47 intercontinental bombers to deliver them. The main bomber force was organized as the Strategic Air Command (SAC), with headquarters in Omaha, Nebraska, in the heart of the continent. SAC was an exclusively American command, with no Canadian participation.

What was cheap and convenient for the Americans was cheap and convenient for the Soviet Union as well, at least relatively speaking. The Soviet Union achieved an atomic bomb in 1949, and a hydrogen bomb in 1953. The USSR had many fewer of both kinds of bombs than did the United States, and until the mid-1950s it lacked the means to deliver them. Finally in the mid- to late 1950s the Soviet Union developed its own force of intercontinental bombers, aircraft that could fly to North America from the Soviet Union and, if they were not shot down, fly back. For the first time in the twentieth century, North America, including Canada, was vulnerable to enemy attack. Naturally as the 1950s wore on, this consideration became more and more important to governments. And in the United States there was a new government.

In 1952 the Americans elected the Second World War hero, and NATO's first supreme commander, Dwight D. Eisenhower, as their president. Eisenhower was an unusual general. He had a vast range of acquaintances around the world, and he had the most extensive experience with and knowledge of Europe of any American president. He understood the implications of the failure to implement the NATO force targets agreed on at Lisbon. He was also concerned that the United States not be dragged into a costly and unproductive arms race. On the one hand, this concern encouraged Eisenhower to lend an interested ear to proposals for weapons control or limitation; on the other, it made him search for ways and means of limiting American defence expenditures.

Eisenhower strictly controlled ordinary American defence costs. A large army cost money, and he could not see the point. Instead he built up American bomber fleets and developed the first generation of operational American missiles. The characteristic military doctrine of the United States under Eisenhower was "massive retaliation." Basically, this doctrine meant that if the Soviet Union crossed the line and invaded Western Europe where there were not enough NATO troops on the ground seriously to oppose it, the Americans would respond where they were superior, in the skies. Because in the 1950s the American atomic bomb stockpile was *ten times* the Soviet Union's, this threat had special force.

Nuclear weapons evolved during the 1950s. On the big end, there was the hydrogen bomb, called "the super" at the time. On the smaller end, there were tactical nuclear weapons that could even be fired by NATO artillery. But the main purpose of nuclear weapons was to act as a threat—to signify what could happen if the Soviet Union or any of its Warsaw Pact allies crossed the line and attacked a NATO country. Atomic bombs and the threat of massive retaliation "deterred" attack. The theory of deterring attack was called deterrence.

Deterrence, then, was something definitive, something final. In the 1950s it depended on American superiority in the air, and in bomb totals. This superiority existed, but it remained relatively abstract. The Canadian government wanted it that way and along with other allies let the Americans know that they did not wish the bomb to appear on display as a likely or ordinary weapon of war. The Americans for their part also regarded atomic deterrence as an ultimate weapon, designed for extreme circumstances.

Canada, the US and North American Defence

Canada's heavy defence expenditures in the 1950s did not just mean the brigade for Korea or the troops the government began to raise for service with NATO. They also entailed the defence of North America. With the Cold War, the Soviet Union was defined as a potential threat to the continent. In the immediate postwar years this threat was mitigated by the fact that Soviets had no way to invade North America, or even seriously threaten it with air power. Even when an atomic bomb was tested by the Soviet Union in 1949, there was still no practical way they could deliver it on a North American target.

The Americans nonetheless worried from time to time, but since their demands were sporadic and not especially serious or costly, they could usually be accommodated. Defence Minister Brooke Claxton, a Canadian nationalist, did not find them especially hard to deal with, or to live with. Claxton recognized the realities of power: the United States needed to defend North America and would do so with or without Canada. Under the circumstances, Claxton concluded, it was better to defend North America as a junior partner than to be completely ignored.

Canada's north, the region above the 60th parallel and the tree line, was more a geographical notion than an economic or political reality. Difficult of access, sparsely populated, over a million and a half square kilometres of snow and ice, with rock and muskeg during the brief summers, northern Canada, the Yukon and Northwest Territories, was home in 1950 to about 25,000 people. The government presence was equally scanty—officials of the Department of Indian Affairs, a few RCMP detachments, the odd prospector or small mining company. Canada had just enough people in the north to maintain sovereignty, and little more.

That was enough as long as the north was considered to be Canada's backyard, far from intruders. In the late 1940s, however, the world was being redefined. Instead of confronting potential enemies across two vast, protective oceans, North America became conscious that the Soviet Union was in fact a neighbour, just across the polar icecap.

By the early 1950s, part of the credibility of the threat of massive retaliation lay in the relative immunity of the United States' Strategic Air Command from enemy attack, and with it the safety of American and incidentally Canadian cities from air attack. In the 1950s this meant protection from bombers. Where roads could not run or ships sail, planes could fly, and by the early 1950s some bombers had a range of 9,500 kilometres, enough to fly from Siberia to North America, and back. However, such flights would take several hours to reach their targets, time enough to arrange for response and defence, or so it was hoped.

The Canadian government had reservations about basing the deterrent in Canada. Canadian reservations were mitigated by an anomalous situation created when, in 1949, Newfoundland joined Canada. As a British colony, Newfoundland was home to a number of American air and naval bases, granted during the Second World War. These bases were on long-term leases, and the leases survived Newfoundland's entry into Confederation. The American bases could and did serve as stations for American bombers, which carried nuclear weapons, and as refuelling points for the Strategic Air Command.

This situation perturbed the Canadian government, but there was little it could do about it. It continued to be nervous and reluctant about allowing the United States to use Canadian space, even aerial space, as if it were its own. Consequently, Canada wished to be consulted about any overflights by American aircraft, a detail that proved to be time-consuming and irritating for the Americans, but which preserved the principle of Canadian sovereignty over its own territory. There was no question, in the final analysis, that the interests of the two countries coincided in case of a Soviet attack, and thus they co-operated in measures designed to detect such an attack.

The deterrent depended on the construction of radar lines in the Canadian north, snaking from east to west across the continent. There were three of these. The Pinetree Line, completed in 1954, ran east to west in the latitude of Kenora, Ontario. The Mid-Canada Line, or McGill Fence, completed in 1957, ran along the 55th parallel. The Distant Early Warning Line or DEW Line, running along the Arctic coast from Alaska to Baffin Island, was also completed in 1957.

Building these radar lines was a massive and expensive undertaking. At first, in the earlier Pinetree Line and Mid-Canada Line, Canadians paid for what was located in Canada. But the DEW Line was too expensive, and there the Canadian government settled for an oversight role, plus the participation on equal terms of Canadian contractors in building the DEW Line stations.

The concern with maintaining Canadian sovereignty while co-operating with the United States in the defence of North America indicates that a strong Canadian nationalism was associated with the Liberal government of the day. Anxious to co-operate with the Americans, the Canadian government was almost as anxious to set limits to that co-operation.

Canada's defence efforts in the 1950s rested on a solid grounding in public opinion, a public opinion that accepted the main tenets of the Cold War and that was, on occasion, militantly anti-Communist. In the United States, the 1950s were characterized by a strikingly powerful and conformist anti-communism, which manifested itself in the phenomenon of McCarthyism, named after the Communist-hunting senator Joseph McCarthy of Wisconsin. McCarthy used congressional committees to persecute people in the United States who he claimed were Communists or Communist sympathizers and who he believed threatened the United States from within. Sometimes his accusations were accurate, but they usually were not, and they were usually made without proof. Yet McCarthy's claims that Communists were rampant in the US government helped to create an atmosphere throughout the country where being accused, without any proof provided, of being a Communist or Communist sympathizer led to hundreds of careers, and sometimes lives, being destroyed. Critics, including Canadians, were not slow to spot the resemblance to the witch-hunts of earlier centuries.

Canadian officials, and most Canadian politicians too, disapproved of the McCarthyite variety of anti-communism. They comforted themselves that such tactics would never be used in Canada. Certainly it is true that anti-communism never became a major political issue in Canada. The Canadian Communist party was not outlawed and managed to maintain a few elected officials in Winnipeg or Toronto. Some trade unions had a strong Communist tinge, like the Mine, Mill and Smelter Workers Union or the Canadian Seamen's Union, which manned Canada's dwindling merchant marine.

The trade unions were probably the fiercest battleground between pro- and anti-Communists. Non-Communist labour leaders in Canada had plenty of experience with Communists during the 1930s and 1940s, and viewed communism as an attempt to harness workers' demands for better treatment and higher wages to Moscow's passing political fancies. There was also pressure from American trade union organizations, much more influenced by McCarthyism than their Canadian counterparts, to get rid of any Communist taint. The Canadian Seamen's Union, to take the best-known example, was violently driven off the Great Lakes by the American Seamen's International Union, with official encouragement from the Canadian government, which winked at the admission to Canada of individuals with a criminal record. Unfortunately, the result was that communism was replaced by gangsterism on the Great Lakes, and another round of struggle followed in the 1960s before labour peace returned to the inland waters.

Canadian society tolerated certain kinds, even unpleasant kinds, of anti-communism because that society was, with unusual unanimity, anti-Communist. The early 1950s witnessed a consensus among Canadians. As an American intelligence report put it in 1953,

> ...the Communist movement in Canada is apparently well organized and disciplined, but it cannot be considered a major threat to the stability and security of the country. US-Canada relations and generally Canada's relations with the rest of the free world are not basically affected by the existence of a Canadian Communist movement.[6]

There was a general agreement about the danger Canada and other countries faced from the Soviet Union and communism, and an agreement that the national government in Ottawa was justified in mobilizing Canadian resources, establishing peacetime military commitments, and linking Canada's defence with that of the United States, at home and abroad. Because of the significance of the perceived external danger, foreign policy and foreign relations were a source of unity among Canadians; and for the moment foreign policy seemed to be less a challenge to Canadians' national unity than a reinforcement to it.

Canadian Foreign Policy, Europe, and the Third World

The limitations of Canadians' perception of an external danger also need to be stressed. Canadians faced toward Europe, and were concerned about the Soviet Union. Thanks to the Korean War and the rearmament that followed, as well as the American adoption of a nuclear deterrence strategy, the boundaries between East and West on the European continent became frozen more or less where they had been in 1949.

Stalin died in March 1953. His comrades in Moscow were relieved to see him go, and his immediate successors, first Georgi Malenkov and then Nikita Khruschchev, experimented with a more flexible policy in Europe, and then with a different policy elsewhere in the world.

Europe first. The Soviet leadership attempted to return to inter-allied discussions on the 1940s model before it was too late. They knew that in order to make NATO work, to provide enough troops for NATO's armies, the West Germans would have to be rearmed. From the Soviet standpoint, it was too late. West and East German states had already been created, though in 1953 they were still under allied and Soviet tutelage. It was obviously only a matter of time until West Germany achieved full independence coupled with military integration in a Western defence force of some kind. The Soviet Union feared an armed, strong West Germany on its doorstep. However, a complicated series of events, including an uprising in East Germany in June 1953, and a coup d'état in Moscow the next month, put paid to any serious initiative the Soviet Union might have taken over Germany.[7] Moscow remained tied to its East German client, while the Western powers, who needed German troops for NATO, finally conceded full independence and membership in NATO to West Germany in 1955.

There were a few small gestures of appeasement by the Soviet Union in this period. Austria, also occupied by the four wartime allies in 1945, was granted independence and neutrality in 1955. The Soviet Union also established diplomatic relations with West Germany and released its remaining German prisoners of war. The Soviet leaders, particularly the flamboyant Khrushchev, emerged from their Kremlin shell and went on tour. Canada's external affairs minister, Pearson, visited the Soviet Union in 1955 and met with Khrushchev, in what he hoped would be a signal for a lessening of tension—détente.

Tensions did lessen in Europe as a result of these efforts. Simultaneously, however, Soviet foreign policy moved around

47

Europe, to a new battleground: the so-called Third World, the under-developed countries of Asia and Africa.

The 1950s was the decade that saw the decline of the old European colonial empires, the continuing decline of Great Britain as a major power, the growing dominance of the United States, Arab-Israeli clashes in the Middle East, and the revival of Europe—to mention only a few areas. The Cold War affected all these problems, but it did not begin them, and, seen in the long term, it sometimes accounted for little more than a detour in trends more powerful than anything the Soviets and Americans could imagine. And Cold War alliances were not enough to overcome manifestations of Canadian anti-Americanism or residual imperial sentiments.

Canadian diplomats, and especially Canada's minister of external affairs, Lester B. Pearson, glimpsed and sometimes grasped the importance of these trends—of anti-colonialism as the British and French empires faltered and fell, of Britain's inability to adjust to a lesser international status, of the constant and dangerous turmoil in the Middle East, where the newly founded State of Israel faced unremitting threats from its Arab neighbours. For Pearson the Cold War was still the most important single phenomenon he had to contend with; but its dangers could be mitigated if the West could prevent the seduction by communism of such powerful forces as anti-colonialism and its corollary, the nationalism of the emerging countries of Asia and Africa.

To avoid this seduction was hard. Some of the most important Western powers, Britain and France, were still substantial colonial powers in 1950. Both the British and the French faced colonial rebellions that were sometimes Communist-led. The Americans focused on the Communist connection, and for expedient, Cold-War reasons were tempted to support the British and French. At the same time, the Americans expected former colonies to fall in line in an international anti-Communist legion—in other words, to accept American political direction. This approach almost invariably provoked skepticism, if not outright defiance. The negative examples the Western powers offered to the newly emerging nations were therefore a disadvantage, a handicap, both in the short term—the Cold War—and in the long term—the adjustment of the international system to meet new and powerful forces that went, we might say, "beyond communism." One might even go a little further and argue that on both sides, Communist and anti-Communist, the Cold War distorted priorities and diverted resources that might have been better spent elsewhere, or at least differently.

Canada's position, the position of the Canadian government and its diplomatic service, on what we would now call "Third World" issues was more ambiguous than the American or the British or the French. Canada wished to establish links to the Third World. But Canada was anti-Communist and wished to avoid doing anything that would strengthen communism. On the contrary, the West must do what it could to weaken communism by offering alternatives to the easy temptations of political revolution and economic overturn. The best way to do this was to hew strictly to a non-Communist rather than an anti-Communist path, to avoid identification with the colonial powers. Equally, prudent policy would avoid the appearance of neo-colonialism, a term that gained some currency in this period. Neo-colonialism meant substituting an informal empire of economic pressure and political direction for the old formal empires governed directly from Europe.

Canada faced some handicaps in implementing such a non-colonial or even anti-colonial strategy. Canada, like the United States, was linked by history, ideology and alliance to the colonial powers. Revolutionary nationalists in the Third World were frequently also revolutionary Communists. Communism promised and delivered a break with the past. Its message and its process were violent and thus apparently—though often deceptively—clear. The Canadian government and the Canadian people took the Cold War seriously, and were bound by sentiment as well as policy, especially to the British. There were limits imposed by Canadian public opinion to what a Canadian government could do. It did not pay politically to be over-subtle.

In the 1950s Canadians not only expected their government to be anti-Communist. They also wanted it to guard the connection to Great Britain, bilaterally, but also through the British Commonwealth, which, of course, included many countries other than Great Britain, a fact that many Canadians had not really absorbed. They wanted to be different from the Americans, but not too different. The American way of life, with its unprecedented material abundance, was deeply admired; and on the whole American political leadership was trusted, especially that of President Eisenhower. The Americans were sometimes excessive, and sometimes bumptious to Canadian eyes, and there remained a residual sense of difference, of distinction, even though the definition of difference fluctuated over time.

The 1950s are remembered as a largely pro-American decade. This was true, up to a point. Canadians thought well of their rich American neighbours and strove to imitate them. American styles,

49

American entertainment, American investment were eagerly pursued. Canadians watched American television, directly or via the government-owned Canadian Broadcasting Corporation. The tone of many American programs and their Canadian imitators was righteous. "Good and evil," in the summation of historian Doug Owram, "were both straightforward and unambiguous."[8]

Yet the pro-Americanism of the period can be exaggerated. The Canadian government kept a concerned eye on the American tendency to act first and ask questions later, if at all. The American embassy for its part regularly reported on Canadian nationalism and warned that Canadians hated, above all, to be taken for granted. An American consul in Toronto, going home after a few years in Canada, went public with his opinion that Canadians were shrilly and unfairly prejudiced against the United States. Canadian universities tended to cherish their British roots more than their American environment. And, of course, the number of British immigrants to Canada soared in this period, extending and even strengthening Canada's trans-Atlantic connections.

Among the least attractive American symbols of the 1950s as far as the Canadian government was concerned was the American secretary of state from 1953 to 1959, John Foster Dulles. Dulles, ironically, owned property in Canada, but his perspective on the country was strictly that of a high-flying New York corporate lawyer, which he was. Canada, Dulles told a Senate committee, was a vast, strategically important hunk of real estate that lay between the United States and the Soviet Union. Its inhabitants should therefore be humoured, but not taken really seriously.

Canada at least was an ally. Dulles was a firm alliance man and ironically also pursued, in a half-hearted way, Article 2 of the North Atlantic Treaty, the Canadian article that provided for more than military co-operation. It was, however, in the Third World where Dulles really made his mark—a negative one. Dulles could not understand how anyone could remain neutral in the great struggle between good and evil, between democracy and communism. Where Pearson attempted to find common ground in relations between Canada and Third World countries, Dulles made it clear that there was only one ground—his.

He recruited some Third World countries to two Asian-based alliances designed to complete the encirclement of the Soviet Union, CENTO and SEATO. In theory the two alliance systems, the Central Treaty Organization and the South-East Asia Treaty Organization, resembled NATO. In fact, they were little more than paper creations designed to create symmetry in American foreign policy, by surrounding the Communist bloc with Western alliances sponsored by the United States. Canada joined neither organization.

Canada did, however, belong to the British Commonwealth of Nations. In the early 1950s the Commonwealth was a much looser grouping than it once had been and included a growing number of former colonies. The United Nations was the second forum in which Canada sought links with developing countries. The UN had been paralyzed by Great-Power quarrels in the early stages of the Cold War, but with the death of Stalin and with the appearance of new, independent countries it seemed useful to turn back to what was, after all, the only universal body on earth. But the UN was universal in theory only: it had stopped admitting new members as the Americans and the Russians blocked the admission of candidates who were seen as too pro-Communist or too pro-Western. In an interesting example of diplomacy, Canada helped break the log jam in 1955, successfully proposing the admission of a slate of trade-offs, Communist, neutral, and pro-Western. The Americans were not pleased, but found it inexpedient to resist.

As a result, many newly independent countries were admitted to the United Nations. These admissions had the advantage of maintaining the United Nations as a near-universal organization. On the other hand, they began to tip the balance in the UN away from the Western powers, which until then had a comfortable and secure majority in the General Assembly, into a much more neutral and sometimes pro-Communist or pro-Soviet orientation.

In securing the admission of new members, the Canadian government accepted that it would annoy the United States and particularly John Foster Dulles. But it was not the Americans who turned out to be Canada's greatest problem among the allies. That spot was reserved for the British with whom, on the whole, relations were both good and close in the 1950s.

The British were a declining power in the 1950s, but the extent of the decline was masked by a return to peacetime prosperity at home and the achievement of a purely British atomic bomb. The British government behaved some of the time as if it were a great power, which was unwise, and some of the time as if it were not. It was most prone to behave as a great power where its remaining colonial empire was concerned, and even with a former possession, such as Egypt. The conflict between these two tendencies in British policy, one pliable and realistic, one muscular and sentimental, came to a head in 1956 in a crisis over the ownership and management of the Suez Canal. In that year, the nationalist Egyptian government seized the predominantly Anglo-French Suez Canal Co, which had operat-

51

ed the canal since 1869. The British and French considered the canal, a narrow, artificial waterway that extended about 160 kilometres through Egypt to join the Mediterranean and Red seas, vital to their commerce in the area and vigorously protested Egypt's action.

At precisely the moment when a crisis was boiling up between Britain and France on the one hand, and Egypt on the other, in the fall of 1956, another crisis occurred, in Hungary. A popular uprising overturned the Communist government and for a time it seemed that Hungary might successfully depart the Soviet bloc. The Soviet leadership hesitated, but finally opted for force, and in November 1956 suppressed the Hungarian revolt using the Red Army.

Just as the Hungarian revolt was about to be quashed, an Anglo-French force invaded Egypt, in collusion and conjunction with an Israeli attack in the Sinai. Canada was at first on the sideline of these great events. The Canadian government was known to disapprove of British plans in the Suez, and so was not consulted. The American government also disapproved, which proved fatal to British and French plans. The United States let it be known that it would not support its allies in any way. A run on the British pound and French franc began, while Arab nations in sympathy with Egypt cut off oil deliveries to Western Europe. NATO was impotent in the crisis with which, in any case, it had no authority to deal. Throughout the crisis, the Soviet Union and its allies vigorously condemned the British, French and Israeli actions and supported the Egyptians.

As the crisis grew, External Affairs Minister Pearson flew back and forth between the UN in New York and Ottawa, advising his colleagues, and calming Prime Minister St. Laurent, who was enraged at the British actions. In Pearson's view, British prime minister Anthony Eden's reference to the United Nations in a speech on October 31 offered a means of escape from what threatened to be a disastrous split in the Western Alliance, and in the Commonwealth.

Pearson envisaged the creation of nothing less than a United Nations military force that would be placed between the combatants, prior to the withdrawal of British, French and Israeli forces. He hoped this proposal would command support among the Afro-Asian states at the United Nations, particularly India. The Indian government's reaction to Pearson's vision was important. India had strongly condemned British actions in Egypt, while remaining practically silent about what was going on in Hungary, an ominous development from a Canadian point of view. Pearson needed Indian co-operation at the United Nations in order to secure support for an international peacekeeping force. At the same time, with British policy an obvious failure, he wished to limit the damage to a country that was, after all, very close to Canada, and held in high regard by a very large number of Canadians. He also needed American co-operation and support. Fortunately, American objectives on this matter were almost the same as Canada's. The damage to the Western alliance, in the American view, must be minimized, and the most expedient way to do this was to adopt Pearson's procedures at the United Nations.

A UN peacekeeping force was authorized, and it included a significant contingent of Canadian troops. It should be emphasized that this Canadian initiative took place within the context of the Cold War, and was explained and even justified by a strategy that sought to keep the Third World at least neutral in the struggle between East and West. To the Canadian government, the Suez Crisis was both an anti-colonial and a Cold War issue, and the course of events showed how close the two trends were to merging. Such a merger of pro-communism and anti-colonialism was to Canadian minds a grave peril. If the Soviet Union were able to sweep all the poor and dispossessed nations of the Third World, they might be able to negate the Western advantage in wealth and weaponry in Europe and ultimately destabilize and even defeat the Western alliance.

The world was changing in 1956, and the Suez crisis was helping it on its way. Suez was an immensely important event in postwar history, a fact that was recognized at the time. Part of Pearson's achievement was to patch matters up, to conceal that the British and French had received a tremendous setback, to restore the harmony of the Western alliance. But the harmony of the West as it had been before 1956—and that can be exaggerated—was never the same again.

The Hungarian revolt, submerged by the drama and urgency of Suez, did not especially engage Canada's diplomacy. Yet it too had consequences, for Canada and for the world. The West accepted the brutal Soviet suppression of the Hungarian revolt in November 1956. It seemed there was little choice, short of all-out war with the Soviet Union. Refugees streamed across Hungary's western border and into transit camps. The Canadian government immediately agreed to admit as many as refugees as it could; by July 1957 33,000 Hungarians had arrived in Canada, the last of over a million immigrants from Europe to arrive since 1947. Like their predecessors and contemporaries, they were strongly anti-Communist, and would play a part in keeping Canada's political balance anti-Communist in the 1960s and 1970s.

The Hungarian revolt also had a specific impact on the Left. Around the world, and in Canada, previously faithful Communists abandoned their cause. The spectacle of Soviet tanks crushing a people's revolt was too striking to ignore; coupled with revelations ear-

53

lier in 1956 about Stalin's criminal rule as Soviet dictator it undermined the moral force, the idealism, of communism. Revelations of official anti-Semitism in the Soviet Union repelled Jewish Communists in Canada, as elsewhere. A "mass exodus" from the Canadian Communist party followed.[9] The Left was not dead, far from it. But the Soviet model was no longer a beacon to visionaries in the same way as it once had been.

These things, long-term trends, were obscured because in 1957 Canada changed governments, from a long-established Liberal regime to a new, Conservative government under a new, charismatic leader, John Diefenbaker. In 1957 Canadians turned inward, and changed their own direction. It is well to remember, however, that many of the changes that came over Canada after 1957 were not of that government's making, or even in the control of Canadians.

NOTES

1. A UN Commission was sent to Korea to supervise elections. Canada was a member of the commission, which triggered an internal crisis in Ottawa between Prime Minister Mackenzie King and his external affairs minister Louis St. Laurent. King, fearing conflict and war, did not want to participate; St. Laurent, who had no such fears and in any case thought such missions were part of Canada's international duty, was agreeable. St. Laurent won, and King, who was about to retire, subsided.
2. Quoted in John English, *The Worldly Years: The Life of Lester Pearson, 1949-1972* (Toronto: Knopf Canada, 1992), 59.
3. A.D.P. Heeney, memorandum to Pearson, top secret, 8 June 1951, *Documents on Canadian External Relations,* volume 17, *1951* (Ottawa: DFAIT, 1996), 1347.
4. "Report of the Second Meeting between Representatives of the Canadian and United States Governments to Assess the World Situation and the Risk of War," 14 June 1951, *DCER,* 17, 1359.
5. Quoted in Doug Owram, *Born at the Right Time: A History of the Baby Boom Generation* (Toronto: University of Toronto Press, 1996), 53.
6. Quoted in Reg Whitaker and Gary Marcuse, *Cold War Canada: The Making of a National Insecurity State, 1945-1957* (Toronto: University of Toronto Press, 1994), 213.
7. V. Zubok and C. Pleshakov, *Inside the Kremlin's Cold War* (Cambridge, Mass: Harvard University Press, 1996), 159-63.
8. Owram, *Born at the Right Time,* 91.
9. Whitaker and Marcuse, *Cold War Canada,* 214-15.

Chapter Four

The Demented Decade, 1957–1968

On June 10, 1957, Canadians trooped to the polls in a federal general election. The Liberals had been in power since 1935, had won five elections in a row, and were expected to win again. To near-universal surprise, they were defeated, and replaced by the Progressive Conservative party under John Diefenbaker. Diefenbaker would remain in power until 1963, and he continued to dominate Canadian politics until he was finally forced out of the Conservative leadership in 1967.

Diefenbaker's vivid and eccentric personal qualities tempted Canadians to personalize their politics and policies, all the more so because his opposite number, the Liberal leader Lester B. Pearson, seemed so unspectacular, homely and normal. This tendency to personalize politics was unlucky for Diefenbaker, and lucky for Pearson and the Liberals. Diefenbaker had to carry the burden of all the adverse events of his six years in power: unhappy events somehow seemed even more unlucky if Diefenbaker were associated with them.

The greatest paradox of Diefenbaker's career was how this prairie Conservative politician, with orthodox anti-Communist and pro-American views of the Cold War, managed to project himself, inside and outside Canada, as a lukewarm ally, anti-American, and soft on Communism. Pearson, on the other hand, about whom many Americans had considerable reservations, became instead the champion of Canada's alliance policy, the "American candidate" in the 1963 federal elections, in which he finally defeated Diefenbaker. Ironically, Pearson again fell out of favour with the Americans when he showed little enthusiasm for their anti-Communist crusade in Vietnam.

There were four main themes in Canada's Cold War policy during this highly personalized, contentious decade. They were all present in Canadian foreign policy before 1957. But before 1957, the various elements of Canadian foreign policy seemed to support one another; after, events made them move into contradiction to one another.

Still basic to Canadian foreign policy and to most Canadians' views of the world throughout 1957-68 was fear of and resistance to communism. This view was embodied in NATO, securely, in terms of public opinion. It was also the foundation of a junior partnership with the Americans in North American air defence. This latter development, which became increasingly prominent in this period, turned out to be much less secure in public affections.

Next, there was the fact that Canada was a small country in terms of people, beside a country with ten times Canada's population. This discrepancy led to what we may call Canada's "small-nation syndrome," and an emphasis on defending Canada's separate identity and national sovereignty. This consideration made Canadians prefer multilateral relations (such as NATO and the United Nations) to bilateral ones (with the United States).

Third, there was focus: "eyes-east." Canadians, overwhelmingly European-derived and reinforced by heavy European immigration in the 1950s, focused on Europe rather than Asia, to the frequent irritation of the Americans who had extensive commitments in Asia.

Finally, there was the nuclear issue, the fact that by 1957 the Western allies led by the United States had come to rely on the "nuclear deterrent"—at first for frightening off the use of Soviet atomic weapons through the threat of massive and overwhelming American retaliation, and then by relying on the sheer destructive power of nuclear weapons to make sure that relations never came to war. Nevertheless, in 1962, the world came close enough to such a catastrophe.

Diefenbaker, Defence, Foreign Policy and a Changing World

Diefenbaker took office at a time when Canada's relative standing in the world was slipping. This slippage occurred for two reasons. First, the nations of Western Europe had recovered economically, so that by 1957 Canada was no longer the third or fourth most important economy on the Western side. Second, the nation closest to Canada, Great Britain, was itself slipping in terms of economic power and political importance. Canada never stood as high in Washington as it did in London, and when, around 1960, Washington became practically the only game in town, Canada's influence and Canada's self-esteem suffered. Diefenbaker, a traditionalist with a highly developed sense of loyalty to Britain and the Commonwealth, was not well equipped to manage the transition.[1]

Nor was he well positioned to understand what was happening to the world in strategic nuclear terms. The question of nuclear defence, of nuclear deterrence, was probably something Diefenbaker had not especially considered. Until the late 1950s the Western alliance relied on the overwhelming American nuclear deterrent, based on unchallenged superiority over the Soviet Union. But in the mid-1950s the Soviet Union acquired aircraft that could easily reach North America's heartland, and in 1957 it demonstrated that it had built and could fire Intercontinental Ballistic Missiles, ICBMs. The Soviets put the world's first satellite, *Sputnik*, into space in October 1957, much to the shock, humiliation and fear of the Americans and of many Canadians. Worse still, the Soviet leader of the day, Nikita Khrushchev, boasted that the Soviet Union had acquired a great effective arsenal of weapons and warheads. The Soviet Union's abundant missiles, he claimed, could not only devastate Western Europe, but could strike NATO's heartland, the continental United States (and, of course, Canada). This boast was not true, and Khrushchev was playing a dangerous and rather stupid game of bluff; but his claims did panic public opinion in North America, including Canada.

Diefenbaker at first approached defence issues, even nuclear defence issues, in a very straightforward and pro-American way. He admired the American president, Dwight D. Eisenhower, and was confident that American policies must be the right ones. In June 1957, within days of assuming office, Diefenbaker approved an air defence arrangement with the United States, that established a joint military command called NORAD—North American Air Defence Command—with headquarters in Colorado Springs, under, naturally, an American general. A Canadian was, however, appointed deputy commander, which occasioned considerable searching of hearts and minds among American officers. The more nationalistic resented even the possibility of foreign command; the more reflective argued that the Canadian would not command very often and that in any case Canadians were practically the same as Americans.

In the 1950s, only Great Britain among the other NATO countries had its own atomic bombs and warheads for missiles, which were just beginning to come into service. Canada had no nuclear weapons of its own, although it did supply large quantities of uranium to the American nuclear program. If atomic weapons were to be based on Canadian territory, they would have to be American. For good reasons, the Americans did not wish to spread the ownership of nuclear weapons even to their allies. The allies recognized that nuclear weapons were useful, but wanted to have some say as to whether, or when, weapons based on their soil would be used. And so a rather complicated system of joint command was evolved, in which both the

Americans and the host country, prospectively including Canada after 1959, had to consent before a nuclear weapon could be armed and fired.

In 1959 Diefenbaker cancelled a Canadian-designed and -built all-weather jet interceptor, the CF-105 or Arrow, which was very expensive, and agreed instead to buy an American anti-aircraft missile system called the BOMARC, which would require nuclear weapons to be effective. The BOMARCs would rise in response to attack by Soviet bombers armed with nuclear weapons, exploding their own warheads near the Soviet planes and "cooking" the enemy weaponry. The fallout from the explosion would drift gently down— probably over Canada. The Americans were originally going to station the BOMARC along their northern border. An alarmed Canadian government persuaded them to move two BOMARC bases north into Canada, so as to defend some of Canada's major cities.

The acceptance of the BOMARC was a plan for nuclear commitment. It was not Canada's only nuclear commitment. Canada in the 1950s accepted NATO's general strategy of relying on nuclear weapons, strategic and tactical, to defend its undermanned forces stationed in Western Europe. Diefenbaker did not differ from this conclusion (the alternative would have been very large permanent armies, which no Western country wanted to pay for). The Canadian government specifically agreed to equip Canada's air division in Europe with nuclear weapons for a strike-reconnaissance role, and Canada's ground troops under NATO with the Honest John ground-to-ground tactical nuclear missile. All these agreements suggest that Diefenbaker was a thoroughly orthodox Cold War warrior, who was not reluctant to accept a fair amount of guidance and co-operation from the United States. The Canadian military and especially the Royal Canadian Air Force enthusiastically advised Diefenbaker to accept the NATO and NORAD commitments. A few diplomats took a contrary view, but they were overruled in Diefenbaker's rush to orthodoxy.

Diefenbaker also accepted the American nuclear doctrine of deterrence, which at this point relied on the unlimited expansion of the American stock of bombs, missiles and bombers. More to the point, it accepted as possible a massive Soviet nuclear strike against the West, and especially North America. Consequently Diefenbaker, like Eisenhower, gave priority to civil defence in the late 1950s—at least until he saw that he was managing to frighten the Canadian population without giving them proportionate reassurance. Newspapers competed with one another in printing radiation maps, while data from nuclear testing—American, Soviet and British at this time—were increasingly public knowledge. The Canadian government constructed a bomb shelter to be used to maintain government in case of attack, and some citizens, too, continued to build shelters. Several larger cities held practise drills with air raid sirens blaring during which citizens were to practise shoring up their dwellings and stocking the goods they would need in the event of a real attack. In Diefenbaker's time in office, insecurity was greater, and fear of nuclear war very great indeed.

There was one area in which Diefenbaker diverged from the political line laid down by the Eisenhower administration. Like his Liberal predecessors, Diefenbaker was careful of Canadian trade interests. A flourishing and profitable export trade was close to the heart of Canadian conceptions of national well-being. Yet trade with Canada's best partner, the United States, produced regular and apparently eternal deficits with Canada importing more from the United States than it exported, while exchanges with Great Britain, Canada's second largest customer, were becoming uncertain in the face of the creation of the European Common Market in 1957. (Great Britain did not immediately join, but it made its first application in 1961.) Meanwhile, subsidized American wheat exports cut into Canadian markets.

The Communist world offered alternative markets, and Canadian trade ministers and their officials had no problem following where profit beckoned. Trucks to China, spare auto parts to Cuba (communized in 1959-61), and most important of all, wheat to the Soviet Union and China all contributed positive dollars to Canada's trading accounts.[2] The United States government was not pleased, but usually did not press matters to the final point of obstruction, even when Canadian subsidiaries of American companies were involved. American policy was to forbid such exports. The Canadian government argued that companies on Canadian soil should obey Canadian, not American law; in other words, American law should not have "extraterritorial" application.

Exports to Communist countries ballooned under Diefenbaker, up from $47 million in 1959 to $247 million in 1960. Canada could thank Communist farm policy for some of the windfall. Shortages of wheat in the Soviet Union and China boosted demand in the two Communist giants. Canadian wheat exports rose by 250% between 1959 and 1965, masking declines in other areas, and ending an eight-year slump in prairie wheat sales.[3] The Soviet Union was by the mid-1960s Canada's fourth-largest customer; Communist China, ranking ninth, was also a serious consumer after the disasters of Mao Zedong's famine-inducing agricultural policy.[4]

There is no evidence that Canadian political foreign policy was directly constrained by considerations of commerce with the Communists. The Eisenhower administration was generally accommodating, while the Kennedy administration actively tried to end what it considered the extraterritorial irritant in Canadian-American relations. The Americans could reflect that Canadian trade with the United States far outweighed trade with the Communists, had any balancing been called for.

Trade was a sign of normalizing relations, and it contributed to a hope that relations with the East Bloc not only could be, but would be, better. Better still, this trade was almost entirely one-way. Though Canada had conceded "most-favoured nation" status—a technical term, meaning the lowest available tariff was applied—to the Soviet Union in 1955 during a visit by Lester B. Pearson to Moscow, the Soviets sent minuscule quantities of exports to Canada throughout the 1950s and 1960s.

Trade with the East did not include any "strategic" items, banned from sale to the Communists by inter-allied agreement. Trade with Western allies did. A Defence Production Sharing Agreement with the United States produced $259 million in American orders for Canadian industry in 1965 alone ($68 million from other countries that same year.)[5] Canada's defence trade contacts with the United States presented a harmonious picture, in which Diefenbaker's agreement in 1959 to buy American anti-aircraft BOMARC missiles was a natural fit.

When Diefenbaker agreed to acquire BOMARCs and to equip Canadian forces in NATO with nuclear weapons there was no reason to expect trouble with the Americans. Then three things happened. The first two were political, even personal. First, the Republican Eisenhower administration was replaced by the Democrats under John F. Kennedy. Second, Diefenbaker made Howar Green, a zealot for nuclear disarmament, his external affairs minister. At almost the same time he made Colonel Douglas Harkness, an orthodox believer in nuclear weapons, defence minister. The third was an apparent change in the public mood in the late 1950s toward nuclear disarmament and disapproval of the West's reliance on nuclear weapons which was manifested in part by the growth of a fledgling peace movement and the start of anti-nuclear weapons demonstrations. This change in mood was amplified by the large volume of correspondence that Diefenbaker received from anti-nuclear skeptics.[6]

What was not apparent, at least to Diefenbaker, who was influenced more by anti-nuclear correspondents than by public opinion polls on this issue, is that those in Canada who set great store on nuclear disarmament were still a minority.

Kennedy was a complete contrast to Diefenbaker. Diefenbaker came from a humble background and had promoted himself by his own intelligence and talents. No-one ever claimed that Diefenbaker's talents included good looks or flashy style. Diefenbaker had little exposure to the world outside Canada, and relied on traditional, "solid" symbols like the monarchy to anchor his worldview. Kennedy was glamorous, well travelled, sophisticated and, though intelligent, had relied on his father's money and influence to make his way in the world. These differences in appearance and background did not pass unnoticed in the press, at least in Canada. How could Diefenbaker, a product of the 1890s, compete in the "Swinging Sixties" with the adored and much younger Kennedy? Diefenbaker wondered too, and did not like what he concluded.

There is no doubt of Diefenbaker's hatred for Kennedy. Canadians are less aware that Kennedy heartily reciprocated. That dislike was awkward, because Kennedy initially rated the prospects for Canadian co-operation highly, and instructed his officials to give greater importance to Canadian-related matters. He had, for example, hoped for Canadian aid in his various schemes for Latin American development, an important aspect of his Cold War strategy, which aimed to fight communism by aid to underdeveloped countries. This aid Diefenbaker rejected, firmly and indignantly, in a meeting with Kennedy in Ottawa in May 1961. That was disappointing for Kennedy, but not especially important. What attracted the American president's attention was a later assertion by Diefenbaker that he had secured an American secret memorandum left behind after a meeting in Ottawa that indicated the Americans would "push" for some of their objectives. Diefenbaker behaved as if he had found a political philosopher's stone, implying that he would use the memo as leverage in some future political confrontation. Diefenbaker's reaction was disproportionate to the cause—so disproportionate that some have since questioned his sanity. The personal incompatibility between Diefenbaker and Kennedy no doubt explains some of the problem; Diefenbaker's belief that Kennedy and his officials took Canada for granted may explain the rest. But when Kennedy learned that Diefenbaker was brandishing a confidential American memorandum, and exaggerating its content, he was furious, and thereafter took his own disproportionate interest in Canadian politics.

Teetering on the Brink

The Kennedy administration had to deal with two of the most dangerous crises between East and West in the postwar period.

The first, the Berlin Crisis, starting late in 1958 and peaking in the summer of 1961, was characterized by threats and sabre-rattling from Soviet leader Khrushchev and an enormous heightening of East-West tension. The root cause of the crisis was the dismal performance of the East German government compared to its West German counterpart. Not only did East Germans enjoy restricted personal and political freedom, their standard of living lagged far behind that of the West. They could see these differences daily in the isolated allied enclave of West Berlin (the three Western powers had consolidated their three occupation sectors of Berlin into West Berlin), to which they migrated in their thousands and eventually hundreds of thousands. To stem the haemorrhage and "solve" the problem of Berlin and Germany, with which no formal post-Second World War peace treaty had yet been signed, Khrushchev in 1958 demanded greater control over West Berlin, and threatened unilateral action to get it. In doing so, he reopened an explosive issue that had remained relatively quiet for nearly a decade. The Western powers firmly rejected Khrushchev's demands and began to mobilize their forces. Tension lessened, but did not end, in the fall of 1959 after Khrushchev agreed to resume negotiations over Berlin and Germany.

During the negotiations the Berlin Crisis continued to simmer. Then early in June 1961, during a meeting with Kennedy, Khrushchev hinted that he would soon sign a peace treaty with East Germany that would recognize East German sovereignty over all Berlin and so involve the end of the Western occupation of the city's western sections. The Soviet threats caused many East Germans to fear that their escape route to the West through West Berlin might soon be cut off. As a result, refugees flooded into the western parts of the city.

The enormous increase in the number of East Germans fleeing to West Berlin provoked a rapid escalation in East-West tension. Both sides intensified their arms build-up, and the Soviet Union broke the unofficial nuclear truce that had prevailed since 1958 by testing a monster fifty-megaton bomb, the largest in history.

The crisis was ultimately ended, though not solved, in mid-August 1961 when the Communist authorities erected the Berlin Wall between the Western and Eastern sectors of the city, cutting off the flow of people from East Berlin to West Berlin. In the streets of Berlin, Russian and American tanks confronted each over a chalk mark that marked the line dividing East Berlin from West Berlin at the crossing point used by occupation forces. The Berlin Wall large-ly ended Berlin's unique four-power status and virtually sealed the last break in the iron curtain. By the end of the year, tension over Berlin had declined. Khrushchev lifted his deadline for signing a peace treaty with East Germany and agreed to discuss disarmament and a nuclear test ban. However, the test-ban talks collapsed almost at once. The United States and Britain feared that the Soviets had stolen a march in the nuclear arms race and thus resumed their own testing of nuclear weapons.

The second great event of this period, the Cuban Missile Crisis of October 1962, was also the result of a Soviet initiative, secret this time, to put nuclear missiles in the recently communized island of Cuba. Cuba was just 140 kilometres from the American coast; if it had nuclear warheads, it could target every American and Canadian city within a 4000-kilometre range. By October the American government had assembled unmistakable evidence that Soviet forces had established missile bases on the island. The American government ordered its naval and air forces to impose a strict quarantine or block-ade around Cuba to prevent Soviet ships that were on their way to the island bearing fresh arms shipments from reaching their desti-nations in Cuba. The world was abruptly brought to the brink of a nuclear war. While a terrified world watched, diplomats desperately sought a peaceful solution. The Americans dramatically presented their proof on television, and in the United Nations. Citizens in large Canadian and American cities, cities they knew would be targeted by Soviet ICBMs in the event of war, debated whether they should try to get out of the cities and if so where should they go—where would they be safe or was there anywhere they would be safe? After ten days, during which the armed forces of both East and West were kept constantly at the alert, the crisis was defused by direct negotiations between Moscow and Washington. The Soviets pulled their missiles out of Cuba, and the United States pledged not to invade Cuba. Some months later, the Americans also dismantled their missile bases in Turkey, which were aimed at targets in the Soviet Union.

Canada was not directly involved in the Berlin Crisis, although the Canadian government viewed its development with anxiety. There was plenty of time for consideration and consultation, factors that appealed to the Canadians. The Canadian role over Berlin was generally supportive, and included a significant increase in Canadian force levels in 1961—just in case.

Cuba, however, was different. Canada had economic interests in Cuba, especially in banking, when revolutionaries under Fidel Castro came to power in that island in 1959. At first Castro's intentions were not manifest, and it was possible until early 1960 to argue that the Cuban Revolution was nationalist at bottom and reformist in practice. If Castro was anti-American, that was because of the historical domination of the island republic by the United States and the dismal record of American-backed politicians ruling the island. When Castro proceeded to nationalize businesses, both Cuban and foreign-owned, he did not immediately proceed against such Canadian enterprises as the Royal Bank or the Bank of Nova Scotia. Confronted with American economic boycotts, Castro proclaimed his intention of getting spare parts for Cuba's American-manufactured machinery in Canada. Canada's trade minister, George Hees, responded with a happy burble that there were no better trading partners anywhere—even as he was advised by the Canadian embassy in Havana that any advantage to Canada was strictly tactical and temporary. And indeed even Canada's banks in Cuba were eventually wound up, though for what the banks considered to be an acceptable price.

In April 1961, the Americans, alarmed by Castro's growing relationship with Moscow and his efforts to foment Communist revolution elsewhere in Latin American, backed the efforts of a group of Cuban exiles who planned to land on the island and overthrow Castro. The attempted landing in the Bay of Pigs failed disastrously, and the United States' involvement produced a good deal of criticism of the Kennedy administration both inside and outside the United States. What is most notable about the Cuban imbroglio, as far as Canada was concerned, was the resulting Canadian skepticism of American advice and American policy toward Latin America. The American government, for its part, was irritated and indignant, not to say contemptuous of the idea that Canada could be better informed or better directed when it came to Latin American policy in general and Cuban policy in particular.

In October 1962, during the Cuban Missile Crisis, the Americans sought the support of their allies. Of these the most reluctant was Diefenbaker, who communicated to public opinion at home and in the United States that he was unenthusiastic and suspicious about the American course of action. Diefenbaker was no enthusiast for Castro but he was also no great fan of American Cuban policy. More generally and more significantly, he resented the fact that on a matter involving possible nuclear war the Americans had acted first and informed later. Consultation, of course, was never in question.

Canadian public opinion did not see matters Diefenbaker's way at all. The West was in danger, the Communists were up to no good in Cuba, and Kennedy had reacted quite properly. The Canadian military did not see things Diefenbaker's way either. His defence minister, Douglas Harkness, quietly authorized bringing Canadian defence forces to the same state of readiness for attack as their American counterparts. The military, on sea and in the air, enthusiastically complied. When Diefenbaker finally climbed on board Kennedy's bandwagon, Canadian opinion was not appeased. His gesture was too little and too late.

Diefenbaker's political position was already weakened by his narrow victory in the Canadian general election of June 1962 in which he was left with only a minority government in Parliament, dependent on the votes of two minor parties, Social Credit and the New Democratic Party, to prevail over the Liberals. In this condition he had to press on with negotiations with the Americans, who wanted Canada to arm the weapons for its air force and army stationed in Europe and the BOMARC missiles in North America with nuclear warheads. The Canadians had already agreed to take the weapons, the Americans argued, and their allies relied on them keeping their word.

The American position was correct. In 1954, 1957 and 1959 the Canadian government had committed itself in Europe and then in North America to policies that required the use of nuclear weapons—by Canadian troops. Most Canadians agreed with this commitment. However, the vocal segment of Canadian opinion that had begun to take the view that the nuclear arms race was suicidal, and nuclear weapons immoral, urged Canada not to countenance by word or deed a policy that might ultimately destroy the world. The anti-nuclear movement commanded support from a broad cross-section of Canadian society, including some prominent Conservatives, outside and inside government. Diefenbaker's secretary of state for external affairs, Howard Green, and Green's undersecretary, Norman Robertson, agreed with the nuclear dissenters.

Diefenbaker, unable to make up his mind or to discern where the greatest political advantage lay, thrashed miserably around over the winter of 1962-3 trying to find a way out of his dilemma. In public, he pretended he had time and that negotiations with the Americans over nuclear weapons were going well. The Americans, losing patience with his frequent and misleading public statements, finally unleashed a weapon of their own. They issued a press release terming the state of negotiations with Canada unsatisfactory, laying bare for all to see the deep disagreement between the Canadian and American governments on the nuclear issue.

A Cabinet crisis followed in Ottawa, as pro-nuclear and anti-nuclear factions in the government did battle. The defence minister, Harkness, resigned, and two others soon followed, expressing lack of confidence in Diefenbaker's defence policy. In Parliament the government was defeated on a non-confidence motion and forced to call a general election for April 8.

Changing Emphasis in Canadian Foreign Policy
In the election campaign, the Opposition Liberals, under Lester Pearson, took a stand on what might be called the first principle of Canada's postwar foreign policy, anti-communism, and the Conservatives on the second, national sovereignty and identity. Anti-nuclear opinion proved to have little electoral force except on the Left. There were other issues in the 1963 election besides foreign policy, the United States, and the Cold War, and Diefenbaker's incompetence in managing them; but 1963 was one of the few Canadian foreign policy elections par excellence.

Before 1962 no one exactly knew what would happen in a time of acute crisis. After the Cuban Missile Crisis it was much clearer. Popular films of the period, *On the Beach, Dr. Strangelove, Fail Safe*, drove home to an uncomfortable audience that the safety of the world depended on the thoughts and actions of a very few people, within a time frame of a very few hours. In each movie, some or all of the earth's population were incinerated or poisoned by nuclear weapons. The CBC contributed its own international incident by staging the TV drama "The Offshore Island," by Marghanita Laski, about the aftermath of a nuclear war in Great Britain and the enforced sterilization of contaminated survivors by their American rescuers. The production was noted and criticized by an American media that was used to seeing East-West differences in an unambiguous black and white. Laski's play—and the CBC's decision to broadcast it—suggest that times were changing.

There *was* a change in Canada's approach to the Cold War in the early to mid-1960s. The Cuban Missile Crisis had afforded a demonstration of what might happen in a real nuclear showdown between East and West. Secrecy, security, the need for effective, concentrated decision making, the overwhelming preponderance of the United States in weaponry, the lack of time—not to mention American nationalism and the sense that the United States had more at risk than any other country—all this meant that the United States would operate in a serious crisis on a blank cheque pre-signed by its allies. The trouble with this new world was that Canada did not fit in at the

top, where the decisions were made, nor did any other national enti-
ty except the two superpowers whose authorities alone could start
(but possibly not stop) a nuclear exchange.

This fact imposed a different kind of dynamic on Canada's
alliances. Canada could and did raise funds, recruit troops and send
largish volunteer forces abroad. These were, it was believed in the
1950s, a kind of ticket of admission to the alliance club presided over
by the United States. Once in the club, there could be speculation,
planning and shared information, right up to but not including the
point when consultation would become necessary. For that there
would not be time.

The crisis of 1962 also demonstrated that the two alliances and
their leaders would not go to war without considerable hesitation.
During the Cuban Missile Crisis the Soviets had the opportunity to
put pressure on the West in Central Europe, and especially in encir-
cled Berlin. They chose not to do so.[7] Both sides, in the aftermath of
the Cuban crisis, drew back and the crisis was quickly followed by
gestures of goodwill. An atmospheric test ban treaty was finally
signed in Moscow in August 1963. While the treaty did not end the
nuclear weapons race it limited the immediate danger to the health
and safety of most of the world's peoples. (Certain countries such as
France, which had recently acquired its own nuclear bomb, declined
to sign the treaty as a sign of their exuberant belief in national sovereignty and unlimited national self-interest. French atomic tests
continued into the 1990s.)

Once the fact of the reduced danger was grasped, there began a
slow deflation of Canada's military policy. Canada under the Liberals
did take nuclear weapons for its armed forces. But the Canadian government thereafter placed less emphasis on those armed forces and
found other priorities for spending money. Because the 1960s were
prosperous and money was abundant, this trend was not at first
noticed; but it is perceptible in proportionately reduced defence bud-
gets from 1963 on. The change in emphasis would not be officially
recognized for some time, or publicly announced until a new prime
minister took the reins of office in 1968.

The Vietnam War

If the United States was both ally and problem in connection with
nuclear weapons, the same was doubly true of the American
involvement in Vietnam.

The Vietnam War was a major episode in the international rival-
ry called the Cold War. In some senses the war was a turning point

in that struggle, though it was not quite what people thought it to be at the time. It had major effects on the Western alliance and on the American capacity to lead that alliance; and it had a major effect on Canadian-American relations. It provoked a protest movement that expressed itself through domestic disorder and civil disobedience in most of the major Western countries, including Canada. In the late 1960s and early 1970s Vietnam was *the* political issue in the United States, and very close to the top of Canada's agenda too. The war seemed to pit young against old, youth culture against tradition, the Baby Boom generation against its seniors. For the first time in a hundred years Canada received an influx of American refugees—up to 100,000 young men who refused to serve in the war and who preferred exile to jail.

Vietnam demonstrates the close linkage between domestic politics, and domestic society as a whole, and foreign relations. It was a period when Canadian nationalism flourished, and took as its symbol and even its rationale American conduct in the Vietnam War. A vocal public opinion in Canada demanded that the Canadian government "do something" about the war. The Canadian government, for its part, believed it could do little about the war, was convinced that the American government would not listen to it, and understood that Canada and the United States had common interests that transcended the war. In examining Canada's diplomacy in this period and on this issue, it should be understood that the Canadian government's objective was to defuse, minimize and distance an important domestic political and cultural phenomenon with which it had little sympathy. The Vietnam War is thus also a case study in the relationship between foreign policy and public opinion.

The Vietnam War went back to an anti-colonial, Communist war against the local colonial power France. French Indochina was a rich colonial belt stretching from the Chinese border to the Gulf of Siam and included three ethnically distinct peoples of Laos, Cambodia and Vietnam. During the Second World War Indochina had been occupied by Japan. When the French returned to their former colony in 1945, they were confronted with a powerful insurrectionary nationalist movement. They had little difficulty in restoring their hold on Cambodia and Laos, but in Vietnam the Japanese war had provided the opportunity for the small but vigorous Communist party to assert its leadership over fragmented nationalist groups. Under their leader, Ho Chi Minh, the Communists achieved a shaky control over the northern part of Vietnam, where they proclaimed a provisional Republic of Vietnam, and began to contest the efforts of the French to re-establish their pre-war position. For nearly a decade Ho's Viet Minh, or League for the Independence of Vietnam, battled French forces, using guerrilla tactics developed by the Chinese Communists. The struggle was terminated in 1954 with a French defeat in a major battle. By this time the Viet Minh held most of northern Vietnam and part of the south as well. If fighting continued, total French defeat was certain, unless France's allies immediately sent troops. Under the circumstances, peace was indicated.

An international conference meeting in Geneva in 1954, where it was trying to wrap up the Korean War, agreed that the Indochina war would be concluded by a cease-fire between the French colonial forces and the Communist insurgents. The French army would withdraw from northern Vietnam, including the colonial capital, Hanoi, and regroup in the south. Vietnam was divided by a cease-fire line and a demilitarized zone along the 17th parallel. Refugees would be allowed to move from north to south, and south to north, according to their preference. International Control Commissions were established for Vietnam, Laos and Cambodia to supervise the cease-fire and the separation of the combatants. The Control Commissions had three members each—the same three members: Poland, representing the Communist bloc, India, representing neutral, Asian interests, and Canada, a Western country.

The cease-fire was the only item at Geneva on which everybody agreed. There were other conclusions of the conference, such as a provision for elections in a few years' time, but not everyone accepted the idea, and even fewer delegations believed fair elections could ever take place. The Vietnamese Communists, the Viet Minh, accepted the terms only under protest, and under pressure from their Soviet and Chinese allies; while anti-Communist Vietnamese made plain their rejection of any settlement that would legitimize the Communists. Both sides went ahead and organized their own states: Communist North Vietnam, under Ho Chi Minh, with its capital in Hanoi, and anti-Communist South Vietnam, under the eccentric and authoritarian Ngo Dinh Diem, with its capital in Saigon. The French lingered in South Vietnam until 1956 but then, pressured by Diem, completely withdrew, leaving the role of sustaining the anti-Communists to Diem's preferred choice, the Americans. The United States government assigned great importance to an authentic local leader able to command respect and affection from his people, and between 1954 and 1961 seem to have sincerely believed that Diem was their man of destiny. The Americans pumped in aid and advice in great quantities.

Canadians pumped in good intentions and plenty of personnel. Over twenty years about a third of Canada's foreign service officers served in Indochina, mostly in Vietnam, and the experience had a considerable effect. Canadians were affected on several levels and of course in different individual ways. Canadians went to Vietnam as representatives of an anti-Communist country, but with firm instructions to be impartial and judicious, and above all to-co-operate with the Indians, whose role as a non-Communist power was prized by the Canadian government. The Canadians returned home from Vietnam entirely unsympathetic to the Communists, and in many cases irritated with their Indian colleagues whose position they characterized as partial and injudicious. (But India, after all, was an Asian power, and closer to the consequences of missteps than Canada was.) As Thomas Delworth, one of the Canadians stationed in Vietnam, later recalled, "Our position within the Control Commission was in a sense not as a paid political broadcaster for the United States but as a power that tried to ensure a sense of balance, a sense of reality in what the Commission was doing or trying to do in relation to what was going on on the ground in Vietnam." That was the official policy of the Canadian government. But reality intruded: "I think for a lot of Canadian foreign service officers it was the first time they had seen communism in operation and they did not like, much less respect, what they saw and it had a profound effect on the formulation of Canadian policy in that period."[8]

In the late 1950s the situation in Indochina, though not happy, was not especially violent. At the end of the decade, however, the Communist government in Hanoi decided that it must move to secure by force the reunification of the country. Accordingly it activated its supporters in the south, and both planned and executed a program of widespread subversion in South Vietnam. These activities were presented as an indigenous rebellion, and in fact for many years well-meaning Westerners were led to believe that the war in South Vietnam sprang from autonomous roots with disaffected South Vietnamese peasants protesting their social and economic grievances against the Diem government.

It was just at this point that John F. Kennedy became president of the United States, in January 1961. Kennedy believed and publicly argued that the preceding administration of Dwight D. Eisenhower was in the process of losing the Cold War, by failing to develop a winning strategy in what was by then being called the Third World, broadly speaking the economically and politically underdeveloped nations of Africa and Asia, including South Vietnam. He did adopt some of Eisenhower's reasoning in accepting that the "fall" of South Vietnam to communism would trigger the fall of other Southeast Asian nations to communism—"like a row of dominos," in a phrase much used at the time. This reasoning was then dignified with the term "the domino theory."

At the time it was Kennedy's charm and ability that dominated the presentation of American objectives, and Kennedy was a determined Cold War warrior. Kennedy represented American wealth, power and self-confidence, and he meant to make these factors count. Vietnam was a test of his resolve, and of American credibility, and Kennedy decided to take up the challenge.

The Diefenbaker government had its problems with John F. Kennedy, but Vietnam was not one of them. At Canadian-American governmental meetings, it was the United States that raised the Vietnam issue, not Canada. The same was initially true of the Pearson government, but in 1964-5, with increasing American intervention in Vietnam, things changed. Prime Minister Pearson was regarded at home as Canada's premier international statesman, as a skilled diplomat, internationally certified by his Nobel prize for peace in 1957. Pearson's external affairs minister, Paul Martin, also had many years' experience in diplomacy and a long acquaintance with senior American diplomats such as Secretary of State Dean Rusk.

Familiarity did not breed co-operation, however. The Canadian government had more and more the sense that the Americans were hurtling down the wrong path in Vietnam, feelings that were deepened by the American-sponsored assassination of South Vietnam's president, Ngo Dinh Diem, in November 1963. And while Pearson could talk fairly freely to John F. Kennedy, he had more difficulty communicating with Kennedy's successor, Texas politician Lyndon B. Johnson, who became president on Kennedy's assassination, also in November 1963.

The two men did not initially get off on the wrong foot, but the cautious Pearson and the backslapping Johnson were not destined to be soulmates. The early signs were promising—agreement on lumber exports, and the very important Canadian-American Autopact, establishing free trade in automotive products, in 1965. Very soon thereafter, in March and April 1965, this early accord came unravelled.

By 1965 much of the South Vietnamese countryside was under Communist control. Terrorism extended into Saigon itself, and the South Vietnamese government was teetering on the brink of collapse. Johnson's officials believed the government could not survive without direct American intervention—by using American air power to bombard the North Vietnamese, and by using American ground troops to bolster the flagging South Vietnamese army. In response, Johnson early in 1965 authorized American bombing raids and landed American troops in large numbers. Unlike the US troops that had gone to South Vietnam under President Kennedy, Johnson's soldiers were to serve directly as fighting troops, not as "advisors" to the South Vietnamese army.

It was just at this point that Pearson chose to make a speech in the United States, at Temple University in Philadelphia. In the speech he expressed general support for the United States, but wondered whether a pause in the bombing might not be appropriate. Johnson exploded and summoned Pearson to a meeting in which the president let his irritation run away with his tongue. Pearson left deeply disturbed, while as far as Johnson was concerned, he would never trust Pearson again. Attempts to restore relations at the topmost level were unsuccessful.

Why did Pearson make the Temple University speech, when its consequences were so negative? The answer almost certainly lies in Pearson's desire to respond to domestic, Canadian opinion. His Liberal government did not have a clear majority in the House of Commons, and Pearson had to be sensitive to the more and more vocal calls from the left wing of his party for him to do something to stop the war in Vietnam. Pearson's speech was a very moderate statement, but it was also essentially foolish. Its reasoning was founded on vain hopes that small concessions by the United States—like stopping temporarily or permanently the bombing of North Vietnam— would induce the Communist side to make concessions as well.

The Canadian government had lent and continued to lend its good offices to several exchanges of views between the United States and North Vietnam. On the first occasion, in 1964, a seasoned Canadian diplomat, Blair Seaborn, was attached to the International Control Commission in Vietnam and travelled back and forth between Hanoi and Saigon bringing American suggestions and North Vietnamese responses. Seaborn's activities bore no fruit, except to confirm the American government in its view that the North would listen—if at all—only to the language of force.

Undaunted, Canada's external affairs minister, Paul Martin, tried again in 1966, sending a retired Canadian diplomat with experience in China, Chester Ronning, to Hanoi to sound out opinion. Martin then summoned William Bundy, the US assistant secretary of state in charge of Far Eastern affairs, to dinner in Ottawa to hear the results. It was not a happy meeting. *"It was entirely clear at the dinner that all the Canadian participants accepted that Ronning had found no sign of 'give' in Hanoi's position,"* Bundy later wrote. In what must have been a low for Canadian-American contacts, Bundy reported his conclusion that:

> It was plain from Martin's manner that he took the failure of the mission as a personal blow.... Martin viewed the mission as a major attempt to achieve a Canadian diplomatic success, and as a major effort to put a feather in his own cap as a contender to succeed Pearson.[9]

If Martin was discredited in American eyes, Pearson himself seems to have learned from the Temple University experience. In June 1965 he told Indian prime minister Shastri that while the "chief Canadian worry lay in possibility of escalation of war...his preference was to make Canadian views known to the US through private talks."[10] There would be no more public eruptions from Pearson. The top levels of the American government, however, paid no further attention to his views on Vietnam, public or private.

The Temple University speech was accepted in Canada as a sign that Canada was distancing itself from American policy, which was true only up to a point. That perception, fed by Johnson's explosive reaction, pleased a segment of Canadian opinion, which in turn raises the question, what was the state of Canadian opinion about the United States and more particularly the United States in relation to the Cold War in the mid-1960s?

The answer, curiously, is not all that different from American opinion about the United States. This had also been the case on the nuclear issue. The Canadian-American border was an information highway, with American issues and commentary speeding north for packaging (sometimes) into Canadian editions, or (more often) consumed raw. Canadians watched American movies, read American periodicals and sat entranced in front of American television.

As Vietnam grew in importance in 1964-5, and especially after President Johnson decided to commit American ground troops to the war, an American anti-war movement was born and speedily grew. Again, Johnson's policies contributed to the growth of an opposition.

Johnson's military advisers promised that victory simply awaited the application of more American force. In response Johnson kept raising the troop levels in Vietnam until they passed 500,000—which exacted a severe political cost at home. The US relied on conscription, the draft, to fill its Cold War military. Most of the time, and certainly between Korea and Vietnam, the draft was accepted as an annoying but marginal interruption that because of plentiful exemptions fell mainly on the uneducated, who were less likely to protest.

Vietnam's demands were so large that Johnson was obliged to tap into the college-educated, a risky business because college youth were both concentrated and vocal. Not surprisingly, the anti-war movement flourished on American university campuses, where students feared they faced a draftable future, Vietnam-bound. Some consulted the recently printed *Manual for Draft-Age Immigrants to Canada* (65,000 copies were sold by 1970) and left for the north. Others stayed and resisted more directly.

Anti-war pressures combined with tensions over race. In 1968 and 1969 the United States was swept by a series of Black riots in several cities across the country and parallel campus riots. Canadians uncomfortably watched Detroit burning just across the river from Windsor, Ontario, while their televisions, tuned often to American stations, reported an unending war in Vietnam and increasing civil disorder in the United States.

The Vietnam War witnessed and to some extent caused the partial disintegration of the consensus that supported Canada's Cold War policy. It stoked the negative perceptions of the vulnerable, bilateral (and American) side of Canada's alliance system, and rendered nearly irrelevant the more popular multilateral side. It concentrated attention on a distant, exotic and above all unfamiliar spot. The United States exported into Canada much of its domestic dissatisfaction with the war. On university campuses the war superseded many of Canada's domestic political issues. Some Canadian Leftists, even though they theoretically welcomed fellow anti-imperialists from the United States, were first puzzled and then annoyed that their American cousins were so little concerned for the nuances that distinguished Canadians from Americans.

Curiously, by the end of the 1960s there were more differences between the two countries than ever. Under liberal governments north and south of the border, both countries had struggled to complete the social welfare state that capitalist wealth and abounding economic growth seemed to have made possible. Lyndon Johnson dreamed of a "Great Society" fuelled by government programs, while Pearson and his Liberals promised to complete the vision of social security that had emerged from the Second World War. But, thanks in part to the Vietnam War, only Pearson succeeded, while Johnson floundered into stalemate, defeat, and finally concession, declining to run again for president in 1968.

Johnson was succeeded after the November elections by the Republican Richard Nixon. Canada too changed governors that year, from the Liberal Lester Pearson to the Liberal Pierre Trudeau. That meant Canada changed generations as well, from a veteran of the First World War to a non-veteran of the Second World War.

An Era Ends

Pearson embodied the continuities in Canadian policy from the beginning of the Cold War to its climax in the 1960s. He brought to the Cold War the memories of the 1930s and the failure of appeasement in the struggle against totalitarianism. He brought the experience of a lifetime in which Europe was the centre of the world's troubles, and Asia a distant if sometimes unavoidable distraction. Pearson had been a founding father of Canada's involvement in the Cold War. Ambassador in Washington, deputy minister in Ottawa, secretary of state for external affairs, Nobel Prize winner and finally prime minister, Pearson had not only shaped but implemented Canada's basic foreign policies since 1945.

No Canadian was more closely identified with the institutions of the Cold War and with the alignments that resulted. Pearson was often identified as pro-American, and his policies were held to flow from that supposed fact.[11] Like most English Canadians of his generation, however, Pearson had ambiguous views of the United States, as Canadians had had of an earlier senior partner, Great Britain. An affable disposition concealed his occasionally waspish perceptions of American institutions and his irritation at American assumptions. On the other hand, Pearson believed American intentions were essentially benign and that in the face of Soviet communism Canada and the United States had very similar interests.

Pearson would have preferred a Western alliance less disproportionately indebted to the United States. That meant an alliance with a strong European foundation, preferably a British-designed and dominated one. Pearson almost certainly felt closer to his British counterparts and contemporaries than to the Americans, in part because of a common education and political tradition, in part because the slippage of British power encouraged a more considerate attitude on the part of British officials.

He also felt closer to the British than to the Europeans. The French as always pursued their own interests, sometimes joined with their allies, and sometimes not. Their record of keeping NATO commitments (always second to whatever interest the French had elsewhere) was not promising. When, in 1966, France's president Charles de Gaulle expelled American and Canadian troops from their NATO bases in France and pulled his country out of NATO's military arm (while staying in on the political side), Pearson mused that it might be time to pull Canadian and American troops out of Europe altogether. But in the end he found new bases in Germany and coped as best he could with the quixotic French president's determination to dismantle his North American ally through his support for Quebec separatism with his "*Vive le Québec libre*" speech in Montreal while on a visit to Canada during Centennial celebrations in 1967.

Like others of his generation, veterans of the First World War, directors of the Second World War, Pearson felt uncomfortable with the Germans, but less uncomfortable with Germany divided and filling an otherwise intolerable gap in NATO's resources.

From time to time, especially as prime minister, Pearson toyed with the notion that Canada might withdraw from NATO or at any rate pull its troops back from their European garrisons. It amused him to drop the idea in front of his subordinates—sometimes senior subordinates—and watch the resultant scurrying. But there was a serious point behind his little joke. As one of the alliance's founders he knew very well that a permanent North American garrison in Europe was not what had been intended. Indeed, President Eisenhower had once observed that if American troops were still in Europe in 1961 the West would have lost the struggle with the Soviet Union. Perhaps, too, Pearson was uncertain whether the benefits Canada received from the relationship were proportionate to the burden it placed on the Canadian taxpayer.

Would NATO make a difference in the long run? On this question there can only be speculation as to Pearson's position or conclusions. Pearson as a historian was conscious of the role of accident and personality in history. He may well have doubted that the "fail-safe" sixties had the means to avoid accidental catastrophe. And if a nuclear holocaust *were* avoided, what then? Did Pearson believe that Western political institutions were strong enough to overcome the dire certainties of Communist rule and the allure of "rational" communism? Like many of his generation, Pearson may have felt that the case to be made against communism was political, not economic; and that economic factors—the fabled plans, efficiency and certainty of totalitarianism—would prevail in the end.

At least Pearson could console himself that these factors had not prevailed in his lifetime. For possibly different reasons, they would not prevail in the lifetime of his successor.

NOTES

1. Canada's influence in London survived the Suez crisis, where Canada was judged to have acted responsibly, even by consider-

able opinion in the British Foreign Office; its influence did not, however, survive Diefenbaker, whose sentimental anglophilia did not compensate for a blundering style of diplomacy.

2. On this point see David Farr, "Prime Minister Trudeau's Opening to the Soviet Union, 1971," appendix A, in J.L. Black and Norman Hillmer, eds., *Nearly Neighbours: Canada and the Soviet Union: From the Cold War to Détente and Beyond* (Kingston, ON: Ronald P. Frye, 1989), 116.

3. *The Canada Year Book, 1967* (Ottawa: Queen's Printer, 1967), 954.

4. Thirty million Chinese may have perished in Mao's "Great Leap Forward" between 1959 and 1961: Jasper Becker, *Hungry Ghosts: Mao's Secret Famine* (New York: The Free Press, 1997).

5. *The Canada Year Book, 1967*. 1182-3. Between 1958 and 1965 $1.174 billion worth of American orders for defence materials were placed in Canada.

6. This point is the subject of a forthcoming thesis by Trish McMahon at the University of Toronto.

7. "Khrushchev shit his pants" at the idea of counterattacking in Berlin, according to one Soviet diplomat, quoted in V. Zubok and C. Pleshakov, *Inside the Kremlin's Cold War From Stalin to Khrushchev* (Cambridge, MA: Harvard University Press, 1996), 266.

8. Thomas Delworth interview, Ottawa, May 1996.

9. USNA, RG 59/CFPF/64-6/1990, William Bundy, Memorandum for the Record, 22 June 1966.

10. Ibid., Ottawa embassy to State Department, 16 June 1965.

11. There is a contrary view, according to which Pearson was an "agent of influence" of Soviet communism, having been recruited at some unknown point in the past to the service of international Bolshevism. This opinion received some slight support from the testimony of an American informer, Elizabeth Bentley, in the 1940s and was believed by, among others, the head of counter-espionage for the American Central Intelligence Agency, James Jesus Angleton: see Tom Mangold, *Cold Warrior: James Jesus Angleton: The CIA's Master Spy Hunter* (New York: Simon & Schuster, 1991), 305.

Chapter Five

Détente and Its Doldrums, 1968–1979

On August 20, 1968, enormous headlines in Western newspapers screamed that the armed forces of the Soviet Union and three of its Warsaw Pact allies had crossed the borders of Czechoslovakia. There was no effective resistance. By nightfall Soviet tank troops had occupied Prague, the Czechoslovak capital. The government was under arrest, its leaders bundled unceremoniously into a plane for Moscow.

In the television age, the Soviet invasion of Czechoslovakia was a nine-days' wonder. There were film crews on the spot, and there were plenty of dramatic confrontations between citizens and invading soldiers, instantly transmitted abroad. As refugees streamed over the western borders of Czechoslovakia into Austria and West Germany, there were humanitarian stories depicting suffering, individual and collective. In Western capitals, statesmen expressed indignation. For a few days, Vietnam was relegated to second place on the evening television news and on the front pages of newspapers.

But it was summer, Labour Day was still ahead, and what, after all, could you expect from the Communists? The Western World had its own worries, its own preoccupations. Some Communists, appalled that the Soviet Union should crush the congenial and humane communism of Czechoslovakia, left the party; but the party was already far down in public opinion and had given up making any serious appeal to the electorate, at least in English-speaking countries. The United States had Vietnam, and if that were not enough, it had racial unrest and urban riots. There were rumours of American student revolutionaries, radicals or "Rads," passing through Canada en route to or from their bombing assignments in "Amerikkka." France had Charles de Gaulle, clinging precariously to power after a spring of student uprisings. Canada had Quebec separatism, in which that same de Gaulle was meddling; and Canada had a new, exciting prime minister, Pierre Elliott Trudeau, triumphantly elected with a majority government at the end of June.

Canada's official reaction to events in Czechoslovakia was ano-dyne. The invasion was "a serious setback to rational dialogue," the government announced. "There's little that we can do," the minister of external affairs told reporters, "or little that we need fear concerning any outbreak of hostilities." Canada would do its part, however. It opened its doors to Czechoslovak refugees, and between September 1968 and March 1969, 11,153 Czechoslovaks came to Canada.

The 1968 Czechoslovak events barely merited the term "crisis" as far as the governments in the West were concerned. "Concerned" probably overstates the case. Practically no one approved what had happened in Czechoslovakia, apart from a few ritual chants emanating from the Communist party of Canada. By 1968 there were so few Communists of the Moscow variety in Canada that it hardly mattered what they said. Their function, if they had any, was to add a few lines of the chorus of approval that Soviet leaders required in return for their financial support of "fraternal" parties. Elsewhere, the Soviet Union's actions were taken to be those of a Great Power exerting control in its own sphere of influence. Its behaviour was deplorable, but it did not threaten any Western interests.

The government of the Soviet Union was pleased. It issued a statement under the name of its leader, Leonid Brezhnev, asserting what came to be called the "Brezhnev Doctrine." Simply put, the doctrine said, "Once Communist, Communist forever." No country could be allowed to backslide from the Socialist Camp, and the Soviet Union had a duty to hold the line. According to what was cheerfully called "Marxist-Leninist science," communism was inevitable, the logical outcome of history. If logic required the occasional application of force, so be it.

The Times They Are A-Changing

There are other ways of looking at the events of 1968. It was a year when great events transcended boundaries, even the Iron Curtain. It was a year of riotous rejoicing by student protesters, in Paris, Mother City of Revolutions, in Germany, in Great Britain, and in the United States. Geriatric governments called out their police and thumped out their responses. Marxism and Marxism-Leninism flourished, though their devotees liked to emphasize that their inspiration came direct from the biblical text of the Communist saints, and not from their corrupt inheritors now in power in Moscow. Canadian radicals followed the fashion, though compared to the full-throated American and French campus revolutions Canada produced only a few pallid puffs of protest. But then in 1968 Canada had the exciting, charismatic and certainly non-geriatric figure of Pierre Trudeau to preoccupy its people.

The effect of these radical currents was to strengthen the Left, to advance the cause of Youth at a time when there were more youths, proportionately, in Canada and other Western countries, than at any previous time. There was, simultaneously, a climate of optimism, combined with deep suspicion. "Mankind today has the knowledge that resources exist to eliminate poverty, illiteracy and disease," The Company of Young Canadians, the government's agency for youth action, proclaimed in 1966.[1] That these ills had not been abolished signalled the failure of the older, governing generation and suggested, powerfully, the irrelevance of that generation's beliefs and modes of conduct. The United States, the shining model of the 1950s, became instead the scapegoat of the 1960s. As a consequence, anti-Americanism became much more widespread, publicly and privately.

Czechoslovakia was the symbol, positive and negative, of the times. In Czechoslovakia, which had endured a peculiarly repressive and obtuse government, old hard-line Communists gave way in 1967 to a new and innovative variety, with Youth apparently in the vanguard. "Socialism with a human face" under its youngish leader Alexander Dubcek offered new hope for communism and thus for the world. The spring of 1968 was dubbed "the Prague spring." Communism and the promise of socialism were young again, exciting again.

Dubcek and his government never got the chance to prove or disprove the idea that communism could be renovated. The answer from Moscow was that it could not. The state interests of the Soviet Union dictated two things. First, the myths of communism must be preserved, and foremost among those myths was the idea that nobody really wanted to leave the Soviet form of communism behind. Second, the fruits of victory in the Second World, the Soviet Empire in Eastern Europe which served, among other things, as a buffer between the Soviet Union and its enemies in the West, must be maintained.

The Canadian government was unmoved by Soviet actions in Czechoslovakia. It shared this reaction with most of its NATO allies. In the Harmel report of 1967, NATO had defined its policy for the 1970s as détente backed up by deterrence. The Soviet incursion into Czechoslovakia was deplorable but not especially surprising. Most important, it did not alter the strategic balance in Europe, and it was not, therefore, any conceivable threat to Canada. Trudeau proved to be cold-bloodedly realistic when it came to questions of the balance of power. He did not believe in the pointless expenditure of hot air, when it was clear that Czechoslovakia's condition would not be improved thereby. Trudeau, Canada's symbol of youth and renewal, thus allowed the previous spring's symbol of hope and renewal to perish with surprising nonchalance.

In 1968, the evidence and exercise of Soviet power were impressive. The Soviet Union had finally built up such a pile of atomic munitions that it had reached strategic equality—parity—with the United States. The Americans now had to negotiate with the Soviet Union equal to equal, and no longer from a position of superior strength. Negotiate they did. Under President Richard Nixon and his foreign policy wizard Dr. Henry Kissinger the United States and the Soviet Union seemed to have established a strategic condominium, a world run by the two superpowers. Brezhnev and Nixon met and talked, and their officials produced a Strategic Arms Limitation Treaty for them to sign in 1972. Effectively, the treaty ratified the status quo, but even that was an advance for a world in which no successful arms limitation treaty had been signed since 1930. This was détente, a soothing word meaning the relaxing of tension. It would be heard frequently over the next twenty years.

It was not a perfect world, but if viewed from the restricted perspective of the two superpowers it was more stable than anything seen since the 1930s. In the Soviet Union of Leonid Brezhnev, the West was dealing with a recognizable negotiating partner. This was so because by 1970 communism was no longer a dynamic ideological or even a political force. The suppression of "socialism with a human face" had guaranteed that. In place of international communism was the Soviet Union, a great and growing military power. Outside the Soviet Empire there were still some who worshipped at Moscow's shrine, but the idols they adored were symbols of power and efficiency and often expediency. Moscow's agents abroad were no longer domestic revolutionaries, honestly deluded, but paid agents.

We know now that the Soviet Union at the beginning of the 1970s was entering late middle age, but that is not generally what observers in the West saw at the time and for years thereafter. They saw, rather, the largest country in the world, 22.4 million square kilometres (8.65 million square miles). They saw a parade-ground country, marching semi-annually through Red Square, bands playing and missiles aloft. They saw a huge economy, 60% the size of that of the United States.[2] They saw that the Soviet Union had caught up to and then surpassed the United States in the production of steel and coal and fertilizer.[3] They saw, also, a stable country, fifty years old and more. It was plainly a country where socialism of one kind or another had worked—worked well enough, at any rate, to allow its "command economy" to construct a military machine four million strong.

There were many kinds of Western observers of the Soviet Union in the 1970s and Canada had most of the assortment. There were professional analysts employed by governments—diplomats and military attachés and intelligence officers. There were journalists passing through Moscow on assignment. There were specialists in commerce—in Canada's case, largely marketers of wheat. And there were "Sovietologists," a term that now seems faintly absurd, specialists in the arcane study of the Soviet system. This latter breed was concentrated in the universities, mostly in political science; they emerged from the universities and into the media in times of crisis to practise their arts. While there were a fair number of Canadian Sovietologists, the study of the Soviet Union was a subject whose intellectual headquarters was just across the border in the American academic complex, easily accessible by visits or phone or simply by watching the American PBS network.

The Soviet Union was never seen in isolation. It had its penumbra of satellites and dependencies. True, its intellectual flock beyond its borders was depleted by successive Soviet depredations of which Czechoslovakia was only the most recent, but defections of the faithful did not mean that Western audiences were lost to subtler forms of manipulation—the manipulation of images, the impression of power, and the appearance of unshakable unity. The Soviet Union's ability to influence the West existed in part because the reputation of the United States had suffered in the 1960s and 1970s, for reasons both internal and external to that country. Internally, the vision of harmony, order and prosperity that had characterized American society in the 1940s and 1950s had become dilapidated as a result of racial conflict, urban unrest and anti-war protests in the 1960s; externally, of course, there was the Vietnam War.

The End of the Vietnam War and the Search for Détente

The Vietnam War had been a godsend to the Soviet Union because of what it did to the United States. Throughout the war, its primary enemy, the American government, was forced to concentrate more and more of its attention and money on Vietnam and to send more and more of its troops to Vietnam. As the war became increasingly unpopular at home, much of the government's attention was turned to controlling dissent on the home front. The Soviets, on the other hand, were never required to send troops, merely supplies, to keep the North Vietnamese going. There was never any danger of the war spreading, because the Americans did not wish to provoke even a Korean-scale war by tempting the Communist Chinese to intervene. This aim was accomplished, with Kissinger applying his subtle diplomacy in the midst of the war to bring Communist China and the United States closer together while widening the gap between Moscow and Peking. By the time Kissinger visited China in 1971 Canada and most other Western powers had recognized the People's Republic and its leader, Chairman Mao Zedong. Such recognition contributed atmospherics but as far as can be seen little else to the eventual Sino-American rapprochement.

In an age of Sino-American concord, the Vietnam War began to seem a vast strategic irrelevance to the American government, as it already had, because of Canada's concentration on Europe, and on domestic policy, to the Canadian government. This does not mean that the war was always a complete irrelevance. Other non-Communist countries in Southeast Asia were quite happy to have the United States holding the tide of revolution at bay, and while South Vietnam and its immediate neighbours fell to the Communists, other, larger countries such as Indonesia went the other way.

The Vietnam War was lost in the early 1970s. The war's unpopularity forced Richard Nixon to curtail American military involvement and then to withdraw from South Vietnam altogether, under a face-saving agreement negotiated in Paris by the invaluable and flexible Kissinger. After a very brief pause, during which Canada was part of a fig-leaf international observer force in South Vietnam, the North Vietnamese defeated the South in a spectacular series of battles in the spring of 1975. Thanks to television, Canadians were able to witness the countdown to final catastrophe, including the fall of the South Vietnamese capital of Saigon, which came on April 30, 1975, with the helicopter evacuation of the American embassy, all faithfully reproduced on the flickering electronic box.

Canada closed its mission in Saigon and, it is said, shipped out bag and baggage—baggage including an official car. Local employees were thoughtfully left behind to the mercies of the incoming Communists. Later, as had happened with Czechoslovakia, Canada opened its doors to Vietnamese escaping communism. By the end of 1979 some 25,000 South Vietnamese had been sponsored for admission to Canada. Many of these refugees came to be known as "boat people" because they had fled from Vietnam to initial shelters in Malaysia and elsewhere in boats that were often small, rickety, and dangerously overcrowded.

The end of the Vietnam War marked the end of an era. It seemed to put paid to the excited doctrines of Cold War confrontation. It altered, decisively, the tone of American politics as it let the air out of the balloon of American omnipotence. It removed the great political issue of the Youth Movement of the late 1960s. Deprived of its focus, the movement, in its American and Canadian phases, floundered. Never organized, drawn together more than its members would have wished to admit by an adult, politically defined issue, Vietnam, the movement subsided, and with it the demonstrations and youth revolts that had characterized campus life from 1965 to 1975. The arrival of the Vietnamese boat people suggested that the issues in Vietnam were not so clear-cut after all, that the Communist government of united Vietnam might not be the salvation that the Left had hoped for. Vietnamese communism was just one more unsatisfactory government in a world that Youth could not hope to move.

Youth was in any case not so young any more. The Baby Boom generation reached its natural limits in the late 1960s. The late sixties and the seventies were a time of shrinking birthrates and falling youth statistics. The Baby Boomers were settling down and, uncertainly at first, they became more conservative. In the late 1970s the results of this trend were still difficult to discern, but they were there. In the meantime the American government, determinedly unadventurous under the Democratic president Jimmy Carter, avoided giving its critics any new issues to complain of, seeking instead a continuation of détente with the Soviet Union.

There is no doubt that the American decision to terminate the Vietnam conflict exacted a price. The price had been foreseen as early as Korea in 1950 and it had bedevilled American policy ever since. By abandoning an ally, even one as chaotic and hapless as South Vietnam, the United States would cast doubt on its "credibility"— that is, its willingness or ability to live up to its word and to defend its other allies around the world. Facing defeat in Vietnam, the United States had to consider the possibility that some or all of its other security arrangements would unravel too.

The Soviet Union's directing circles seem to have drawn this conclusion. There was an opportunity to put conclusion into practice even before the Vietnam War ended. In the spring of 1974 one of the weakest NATO allies, Portugal, had finally overthrown its aged and faltering dictatorship, a dictatorship that had been embroiled for years in unpopular colonial wars in Portugal's colonies in Africa. There was chaos in Lisbon, where Communists and pro-Communists jockeyed for power. Meanwhile in the colonies, pro-Communist Portuguese facilitated the transfer of power in Angola and

Mozambique to local Communist factions. Though Portugal finally established a functioning democracy and remained in NATO, its ex-colonies inherited instead endless war between rival political contingents that drew on East and West for material support.

Extension of Soviet influence into Africa (it also popped up in, successively, Somalia and Ethiopia) was matched by the expansion of the Soviet navy. Now Soviet nuclear submarines patrolled the coasts of North America, while the Red surface fleet acquired an ocean-going capability. All this activity occurred in the age of détente, the relaxing of tension, which suggests that there was a problem with the meaning of the word.

As there was. On the Western side, détente was a policy of hope. It was both an object and an instrument. Avoiding war, avoiding near-war, avoiding even the danger of war meant creating a more "normal" international climate in which a common interest in peace and its fruits could be developed. The Soviet side saw détente as more in the nature of a pause, which would allow the Soviet Union to increase its strength without incurring any special costs. The West needed détente because it had lost its way after Vietnam and was negotiating from weakness. Victory in Vietnam showed that communism had a natural affinity with the underdeveloped nations, with the Third World. This affinity was shown by the predominance of pro-Communist or at least pro-Soviet views in many Third World countries, as reflected in their anti-Western utterances and votes in such forums as the United Nations. In the meantime, the West still needed to trade and invest, which would also increase the Soviet Union's strength, absolutely and relatively.[4]

There was one other factor that reinforced the Soviet Union's optimistic view of itself and its future. In the early 1970s a cartel of oil-producing nations, in part taking advantage of the United States' preoccupation with Vietnam, broke the stranglehold of Western oil companies on the production and pricing of oil. This was in some respects a natural and inevitable development. The United States, which had been the largest producer *and* consumer of oil, was by the 1970s only the largest consumer. The largest producing countries were Saudi Arabia and other Middle Eastern states. Under Saudi leadership, the petro-states got together in OPEC, the Organization of Petroleum Exporting Countries, and insisted on raising the price of oil. They raised it, in fact, from roughly $3.50 a barrel in 1972 to $12.00 a barrel by 1976, and still it rose.

The economies of the West, dependent on petroleum-derived energy and petroleum-based products ranging from records, to raincoats, to gasoline, were disrupted for much of the 1970s. Long line-ups at the gas pumps and rising prices for the gas people lined up to get became commonplace. Prices for products based on petroleum steadily rose. With inflation rampant, Western governments had to face domestic economic discontent of a kind they had not seen since the Great Depression of the 1930s. The West did not approach the problem as a unit and had no mechanism for doing so. The terms of NATO, the political bargain made in 1949, did not specify economic consultation, and this lack left the various Western powers free to pursue their own self-interest, which was often very narrowly defined.

As far as Canada was concerned there was a silver, lucrative lining in the dark petroleum cloud. Canada was a petroleum exporter. Oil and natural gas sales to the United States kept part of the Canadian economy buoyant through the 1970s even while the other part struggled with sky-high inflation and rocketing interest rates.

The Soviet Union was a huge petroleum producer. While Western petroleum reserves were declining in the 1960s and 1970s, Soviet geologists discovered more and more oil and natural gas. The Soviet Union was not affected by price rises elsewhere, except that it could use its oil and gas to bind its allies more closely and sell the surplus for useful Western currency. With petroleum as its magic wand, the Soviet Union could simply buy what it needed in Western technology—effectively injecting itself with twenty years of Western technical progress.

Strategy, politics and economics all conspired to inflate the image of the Soviet Union at a time when the West looked increasingly depleted, divided and dilapidated. Even the most stalwart Cold War warriors were disheartened at the contradictions and confusions of Western policy and the apparent lack of vision and resolution in the United States.

Trudeau, Defence and Foreign Policy

These divisions of Western opinion were all faithfully reflected in Canadian policy debates at this time. There were those who cleaved to the old Cold War faith and argued that Canada should shape its international policies with an eye to a common Western interest. In their eyes, the ultimate objectives of the Soviet Union remained the same, and must be met through the constructive solidarity of Western nations, and especially the NATO allies.

There were, on the other hand, those who argued that the Soviet danger had abated, and that the Soviet Union under its post-Stalin and post-Khrushchev leaders did not represent a serious threat to

Western interests. Though the Soviet Union might be rough and crude and unpleasant in many of its aspects, the opportunity existed to abate its appetites, or to satisfy them by means other than confrontation or containment. "Positive engagement" was the watchword of this species of opinion.

It is tempting in retrospect to argue that the second opinion had more to commend it than the first. The Soviet Union did not turn out to be the threat that alarmists, daunted by its rockets and ships, claimed. After all, those rockets and ships and the soldiers and sailors who manned them ultimately turned out to be rooted in a shallow and infertile economy, and finally shrivelled in the sun of economic misfortune. But it is not that the "engagers," or "appeasers" as we might call them, were not also impressed by the might of the Soviet Union. More than the continuing Cold War warriors, they accepted the legitimacy of Soviet society, and assumed that it would be a perpetual neighbour of the West in the international arena. Far better that it be a well-disposed neighbour, in whose intentions and behaviour it was possible to have some confidence.

The Cold War warriors faced serious handicaps in their arguments, some of them self-generated. Perhaps most important, there was weariness. The Cold War had been on for twenty years. The West had been stirred to mobilization and containment by Stalin in the 1940s and the memory of Stalin was sufficient to keep containment vivid into the 1960s. The emotional peak of the nuclear arms race, coupled with the Cuban Missile Crisis and followed by the Nuclear Test Ban Treaty of 1963, had passed, while the American domestic struggle over Vietnam cast doubt on the quality and integrity of American leadership in the Cold War.

That leadership was already regarded skeptically in Canada because of the Canadian perception that the US-allied relationship was not perfectly reciprocal. The United States led but did not listen, from the Canadian point of view, and that fact, true in the lop-sided bilateral relationship, was also true when it came to multilateral organs, like NATO.

If there was fatigue with the moral pitch required to sustain the Cold War, there was also a kind of international disenchantment specific to Canada, which fed into the disillusionment with American leadership. Canadians had willingly accepted the international responsibilities laid down by Louis St. Laurent in 1947 and echoed by Canadian diplomats ever since. When Lester Pearson as external affairs minister won the Nobel Peace Prize this was seen as a case of virtue appropriately rewarded. Pearson won his prize for making possible a United Nations peacekeeping force to stand between Israel and its enemies in the Middle East. It was a force that the Egyptians agreed to receive on their soil and, ultimately, on their terms. That force, UNEF, lasted for almost eleven years, but when the Egyptians decided that the time had come to invade Israel one more time they unceremoniously kicked out UNEF in 1967, reserving the Canadians for particular abuse and ill-treatment.

This event, coupled with a general decline in Canada's overall international standing, encouraged a retreat from foreign adventures. Canada had plenty of problems and other priorities in the 1960s, priorities that even Pearson recognized by cutting back on Canada's defence budget. It was this mood of disillusionment and disenchantment that was caught by Pearson's successor as leader of the Canadian Liberal party and prime minister, Pierre Trudeau. "No more helpful fixers," a scornful remark attributed to Trudeau, and referring to Pearson's indefatigable international involvements, became the watchword of the new generation that was following Trudeau into office in 1968.

Trudeau had views on foreign policy. He had been skeptical of the shrill anti-communism that had characterized the Cold War of the early 1950s. He had even featured on an American blacklist of suspected pro-Communists and like many intellectuals of his generation he had only contempt for the McCarthyism that had disfigured American public life. Trudeau was not pro-Communist, but he was unconvinced by and even doubtful of the means used to resist the Soviet Union. He wondered if the Soviet Union was the proper focus for Canadian policy, and whether the national interest might not be better deployed elsewhere.

In 1968-9 he put the Canadian foreign affairs and defence bureaucracies through an intellectual convulsion by demanding that they examine Canada's security and alliance policies using the strict test of the Canadian national interest. After many internal clashes, both among bureaucrats and between the prime minister and unwilling external affairs and defence hierarchies, the matter was brought forward for discussion and debate by the Cabinet in March 1969.

The debate in Cabinet was in some respects a debate between new and old, between youth and experience. For the younger members of the Cabinet, the Cold War was at best obsolete, at worst a means of enforcing subservience to an irrational American preoccupation with communism. For this group of ministers, the United States filled the horizon, while the Soviet Union dwindled in menace and significance. For the more traditional ministers, including the ministers of external affairs and national defence, the Cold War still defined the world outside Canada, the Soviet Union was still a menace, and Canadians must still accept some of the responsibility for resisting it, using the means already to hand—the NATO alliance.

Cabinet discussions were comprehensive. "By noon we were aligned," one minister remembered, "and by five o'clock we were in NATO." How much in NATO? The answer was, effectively, 50 per cent. Canada's overseas garrison was cut in half. It was a statement, and, obviously, a gesture. In a half-hearted manner Canada was saying that a military alliance, NATO, while not completely irrelevant, especially as a political bridge to Europe, was no longer as strategically important as it once had been, and that force reductions, contributing to détente, were a better provision for the future.

This was a decision that had to be explained to Canada's allies as well as to Canadians. Canadians received the decision with relative equanimity, reflecting the general opinion that the Cold War, especially in Europe, no longer posed such an urgent danger that a large Canadian response was required.

The allies were upset. The Germans, on whose soil the Canadian bases in Europe were located, had legitimate grounds for complaint. The German foreign minister even passed through Ottawa at the time the Canadian decisions were being taken, and was not consulted, a foolish and on the whole pointless omission by the Canadian government. The British, who specialized in unilateral actions where their own interests were concerned, were more vocal and abusive than the Germans. The Americans were in a different position. Trudeau had consulted Richard Nixon, and Nixon had not objected—the only allied leader who had a chance to make his opinion count. But for the sake of the alliance the American delegates to NATO joined in a general if muted show of regret if not outright indignation.[5]

The NATO allies were not overwhelmingly concerned at the military loss the withdrawal of some Canadian troops represented. There was concern that NATO's solidarity had been damaged, and that the credibility of the alliance in negotiations with the Soviet Union had been compromised. But—and this had become official NATO doctrine by this point—those negotiations should lead to détente, a détente that would recognize the stability of frontiers in Europe. Czechoslovakia's experience the year before was unfortunate, but it could be borne in view of the greater good to be expected from détente.

In 1970 the Trudeau government published a series of booklets, *Foreign Policy for Canadians*, to tell the country that the government intended to conduct foreign policy in the national interest, with rather more emphasis on the economy and trade and rather less on security and defence. Critics of the government's policy statements, and they included former Prime Minister Lester Pearson, missed the point that Canada's foreign policy had always been intended to reflect the national interest. Only the proportions in the mix had changed and, it turned out, not by all that much.

Trudeau was determined to add his mite to détente. One avenue was recognition of Communist China, which occurred after lengthy negotiations in 1970.[6] Another was the cultivation of closer relations with the Soviet Union. A visit to Moscow was scheduled for October 1970, only to be abruptly postponed when Canada faced an internal terrorist crisis at the beginning of that month. The event did not make Trudeau look warmly on nationalist-separatists, which caused him some problems when he came face to face with the Soviet Union's nationalities problem the next year.

The rescheduled visit took place in May 1971. The Soviet reception was warm and the usual generally meaningless agreements were signed by Trudeau and Brezhnev. On tour in Kiev, capital of Ukraine, Trudeau let slip that he had no sympathy for "anyone who breaks the law in order to assert his nationalism," a clear reference back to Canada, but also a sign of the times: Trudeau accepted the legitimacy and durability of the Soviet Union as did virtually any and all Western leaders of the period. It was, nevertheless, an impolitic remark.

Ukrainians were not the only ones displeased at Trudeau's comments and actions in the Soviet Union. Suggestions that Canada was seeking relief from the overwhelming reality of the United States did not sit well either with the press at home or in the United States. Was Trudeau seriously suggesting that the Soviet Union was equivalent to the United States, or that Canada was balanced between its neighbour to the North and its neighbour to the South? There was, in fact, no serious prospect of a change in policy, but Trudeau hoped a change in *tone* might help.

The visit was returned by the Soviet prime minister, Alexei Kosygin, in October 1971. Kosygin was probably the best of the Soviet leadership group, and was respectfully remembered by the Canadians he met as intelligent and straightforward. Yet a few minor bilateral matters apart, and always excepting wheat sales, which were already firmly established, there was nothing much to be said or done in Canadian-Soviet relations.

What did it all mean? A visit to Moscow allowed Trudeau to suggest a difference in approach or attitude to the Soviet Union, as compared to the past and as compared to the views of the United States. But acceptance of the fact of the Soviet Union and the exchanges of pleasant words had little but atmospheric effect. The main Soviet interests in the West were the United States, and exploration of any possible divisions between the Americans and their allies. Sometimes if Soviet-American relations were frosty or unproductive, the Soviets would signify as much by increased cordiality toward the Canadians. It was little enough; and it was all.

In the 1970s, Canadian-Soviet relations were overshadowed by the general pursuit of détente by the two superpowers, and in particular by the negotiations for arms reduction in Europe, the so-called Multilateral Balanced Force Reduction talks, or MBFR.[7] More important, and greatly desired by the Soviets, was another set of negotiations, the Conference on Security and Co-operation in Europe (CSCE), held in Helsinki, Finland.

The background to the CSCE lay in the desire of the Western Europeans for a normalized relationship, as far as that was possible, with the Soviet Union and its satellites. This desire was perceptible in NATO policies as early as 1967, and turned on the one hand into "positive engagement" and on the other into West Germany's "eastern policy," the *Ostpolitik*, which aimed to cultivate significant and durable links to the Communist countries of Eastern Europe.

All these approaches, especially the CSCE, suited Canada's version of détente under Trudeau, and they enabled the Trudeau government to engage the support of the differing factions that sought to tap Canada's policy ever so slightly to the right, or to the left.

The CSCE, as far as the Soviet Union was concerned, was about boundaries and legitimacy. It would be a substitute for the peace conference and general peace treaty that Europe had never had. It would, in other words, recognize and perpetuate the division of Europe. The Western powers for their part accepted that they were not about to do anything about Soviet domination of Eastern Europe. Recognizing the East was thus no more than recognizing the inevitable, the more so because the Soviet Union seemed to have established itself for the indefinite future.

In return for Western recognition, the Soviets were willing to talk about such subjects as human rights, which to some Western diplomats, including the Canadians, suggested an opportunity. According to Tom Delworth, the Canadian representative at the CSCE,

> I think that we saw in détente an opportunity to make a whole lot of agreements work with the Soviet Union and its allies in Eastern

Europe, where these had been pretty formalistic, ritualistic, things before. I'm talking about human contacts agreements, consular agreements, family reunification agreements. We saw in détente an opportunity to do a lot of things in the security field of course, but we felt that there was a very close connection between broad overarching security problems, on one hand, and public perceptions of détente on the other. We felt that if détente was not seen to have concrete specific meaning for citizens in our countries, and indeed in the Eastern European countries it could be a fashionable policy for maybe two or three years, but would ultimately fade into the background because it was not underpinned sufficiently in the desires of populations.[8]

The CSCE talks were also an opportunity for the Canadians to re-establish their credibility as constructive and supportive members of NATO, after the unilateral force reduction of 1969. Canada's support for the talks entailed a delicate balancing act. The United States (more accurately its secretary of state, Henry Kissinger, who gave more importance to power than to morality in foreign affairs) was more reluctant than the Europeans to engage in the CSCE, mostly because of its human rights dimension, while the Europeans and especially the Germans valued it for precisely that reason, a reason that the Canadians shared.

The Helsinki Final Act, signed in 1975, was a carefully nuanced document. The Soviets did not get the immovable frontiers they wanted, but won instead references to peaceful change of boundaries. They did not get a "substitute peace treaty," though the language of the document was sufficiently obscure that they could represent it as such. Delworth concluded,

I don't think they had read the final act, not in terms of its detailed words, which are pretty opaque at times, the result of compromised negotiation, but the general impact of the words of the final act, and the philosophy that underpins the whole document, is the philosophy of change, not rigidity and no change.[9]

What did the CSCE mean? The human rights effects of the Helsinki Final Act were long in coming. The West was not going to insist on reforms in the Soviet bloc, but it had signalled that it had not lost interest in the subject. The West's moral case turned on the fact that its human rights practices were immeasurably superior to those of the Soviet Union. To lose sight of the contrast was to some degree to lose sight of one of the major causes of the Cold War.

That human rights were present in the Helsinki document set a standard, more honoured in the breach than the observance for a long time, that pointed up the contrast between lofty principle and sordid practice for the peoples of Eastern Europe. It was a belated response to the brutal suppression of the Prague Spring in 1968.

There was, however, a difference between the mid-1960s and the mid-1970s. In 1967 or 1968, "reform" in European terms might have meant a turn to the Left, to Eurocommunism (a term of the time) or to "reform communism," à la Prague. By 1975 or 1976 "reform" had shed the notion that a Communist road was possible, that there was a compromise between communism and human rights that could still be found. Wherever Helsinki and the CSCE pointed, it was away from communism.

For a while, it seemed that they pointed away from the Cold War as well. It was just at that point that Brezhnev and company undertook to remind the West why there had been a Cold War in the first place.

NOTES

1. Quoted in Doug Owram, *Born at the Right Time: A History of the Baby Boom Generation* (Toronto: University of Toronto Press, 1996), 280.
2. According to the American Central Intelligence Agency. The estimate applies to the 1970s.
3. A point made by Martin Walker, *The Cold War: A History* (Toronto: Stoddart Publishing, 1994), 234.
4. On this subject, I favour the analysis of Martin Malia in *The Soviet Tragedy: A History of Socialism in Russia, 1917-1991* (New York: The Free Press, 1994), 376-7. Malia stresses the lawless nature of Soviet society, and its reliance on force rather than consent.
5. There is an amusing sidebar to these events. In 1966 de Gaulle had pulled French troops out of NATO's military structure; some allies as a result decided that Canada was following de Gaulle, who was by then the mortal enemy of Canadian unity and of Pierre Trudeau.
6. See B. Michael Frolic, "The Trudeau Initiative," in Paul M. Evans and B. Michael Frolic, eds., *Reluctant Adversaries: Canada and the People's Republic of China, 1949-1970* (Toronto: University of Toronto Press, 1991), 189-216.
7. Lasting sixteen years, the MBFR talks ended in stalemate in 1984.
8. Tom Delworth interview, Toronto, October 1996.
9. Ibid.

Chapter Six

Blindman's Bluff:
The Cold War Ends,
1979–1991

The 1980s were the best of times and the worst of times. The worst came first, and once again the initiative did not lie with the West.

In December 1979 the Soviet Union sent troops into its mountainous, fractious neighbour Afghanistan. Muslims and Communist factions, some pro-Soviet Union and some not, had for some time been battling for control of the government. In a 1978 coup the pro-Communist Hafizullah Amin had assumed power but by 1979 his government was floundering, unpopular and divided. Ostensibly at Amin's request, the Soviets staged a massive military airlift into Kabul, the capital of Afghanistan. Within a few days, Soviet troops murdered Amin and replaced him with a more biddable leader.

The decision to invade Afghanistan was taken by a small group of high Soviet officials, most important the Soviet president, Leonid Brezhnev. The invasion represented the high tide of confidence in the Soviet Union's future. Afghanistan, Brezhnev and his cronies told one another, was not Vietnam. There were no jungles in Afghanistan, nor was that country at the wrong end of a 8000-kilometre (5000-mile) supply line as Vietnam had been for the Americans. Rather, it was right up against Soviet Central Asia. Nor was the Soviet Union like the United States. As the events of the 1970s in Asia and Africa showed, the Soviet Union had history on its side; the United States did not. The Americans had been defeated in Vietnam, and had been obliged to recognize Soviet strategic parity and hence equality. Where the Americans had faltered, the Soviet Union had gone from triumph to triumph, intervening in improbably distant places like Angola and Ethiopia, using Cuban troops obtained from that island's Communist dictator, Fidel Castro. As if to confirm the Soviet judgement of the United States, the Americans' principal ally in the region of Afghanistan, neighbouring Iran, earlier in 1979 had succumbed to an Islamic revolution and, as if to symbolize American weakness, the US embassy in the Iranian capital had been stormed and American diplomats imprisoned by the revolutionaries.

These events had reverberations in Ottawa. The Progressive Conservative government of Joe Clark, elected with a minority in the House of Commons in May 1979, struggled to come to the help of its neighbour. As far as Iran was concerned, the help was practical and effective. Canadian diplomats in Iran for some weeks sheltered some of their fugitive American counterparts who had managed to avoid being taken prisoner. The Canadian embassy was then closed and evacuated, with the Americans among the evacuees. For US president Jimmy Carter the escape from Iran of some of his diplomats was rare good news in a bleak season. It helped him overcome his disappointment with Canadian behaviour over Afghanistan.

Carter countered Soviet aggression in Afghanistan by banning American grain exports to the Soviet Union, seeking to hit the Soviets in their vulnerable breadbasket. He also announced that the United States would boycott the forthcoming Moscow Olympics, scheduled for the summer of 1980. Carter sought support from his allies, and found that support heavily qualified.

Joe Clark agreed to the Olympic boycott. Canadian athletes would be extremely disappointed and would protest, but they had few votes and there were in any case few economic interests at stake. If Canada missed out on competing with the steroid-stimulated behemoths of the East Bloc in one Olympics, that was a loss that could be borne. But grain was serious business. Western Canada depended on wheat exports to the East Bloc. The United States had a history of cutting into Canadian grain sales through its various agricultural subsidy programs. Where grain was concerned there was little fellow-feeling across the 49th parallel.

The best Clark could manage was a compromise. Canada would not terminate its grain sales to the Soviet Union, but it would undertake not to sell more, not to replace lost American supplies. In return, the United States had to agree not to undercut existing Canadian sales in other vulnerable and important Canadian markets, such as mainland China. Clark also ended Aeroflot (the Soviet airline) flights into Montreal and suspended cultural exchanges—balancing on the intellectual side his actions in the athletic department.

Trudeau Returns

And then Clark was gone, swept away by his own political ineptitude, and the Liberals were back with a majority government in the general election of February 1980. "Welcome to the 1980s," Pierre

Trudeau told a television audience, which could contemplate four more years of Liberal rule, with Trudeau as prime minister.

The return of Trudeau at this juncture had serious implications for Canadian policy in the Cold War. In the 1970s, Trudeau had witnessed an apparent thaw in East-West relations. The frontier between communism and capitalism in Europe had not shifted. Where the Cold War was concerned, Trudeau took the long view, that the East-West division of 1945 was, in effect, permanent and that stability would be its own reward. Canada's recent reduced contribution to NATO could be justified as a down payment on stability. The Cold War was, as an American historian observed at the time, a "Long Peace," a state of strategic equilibrium.

As far as Trudeau was concerned, what the Soviet Union did on its side of the line was its own business. That applied to Eastern Europe, as in the case of the invasion of Czechoslovakia in 1968, and it applied as well to Afghanistan. Despite previously good relations with American president Jimmy Carter, Trudeau was scornful of Carter's attempts to counter Brezhnev's employment of Soviet power. "What has the US done to hurt itself lately?" the Prime Minister asked, soon after returning to office.[1]

Trudeau wanted to end the Olympic boycott and escape any co-operation over grain sales, but he was persuaded that American reaction would be too severe. Carter's boycott required some co-operation with his allies, and by and large he did not get it. His other actions in response to Soviet expansion received almost no support.

The European allies, especially Germany which by 1980 was the dominant European partner in NATO, were disturbed by another of Brezhnev's initiatives, the deployment of medium-range Soviet missiles, the SS-20s, in Eastern Europe. These missiles could upset the strategic balance in Europe, negate the American nuclear deterrent, and place the European pillar of NATO under threat. The allies asked for, and got, a NATO commitment to try to negotiate the SS-20s out of Eastern Europe. If the Soviets would not co-operate, NATO would threaten to deploy countervailing American missiles in Europe—the Pershing and the Cruise. NATO's approach was a carrot and stick proposition, or as the jargon of the day called it, a "Two-Track decision," one track leading back to détente, the other toward a renewed arms race.

American rearmament began under Carter, but it was amplified and expanded under his Republican successor, Ronald Reagan. Reagan in his campaign for the presidency in 1980 drew on an American perception that the United States was falling behind, was losing the Cold War. He proposed to expand American armaments, and when he took office in January 1981, he did just that. He went further, in 1983, proposing an American technological umbrella that would intercept anything the Soviets could throw at the United States, thereby cancelling the Soviet Union's painfully achieved strategic parity with the Americans. This was Reagan's Strategic Defense Initiative, SDI, also labelled Star Wars because of its showy high-tech presentation and, possibly, its science-fiction assumptions.

Reagan left participation in SDI's costs and benefits up to the allies, and Trudeau's reaction to this phase of American rearmament was predictably negative. He was not negative where the Two-Track decision was concerned. Canada participated in the Two-Track decision, and was bound by it. The Two-Track decision required the emplacement of credible American missiles in Europe, and the nominee was the Cruise missile, a pilotless weapon that could sail under existing missile defences and take out Soviet targets.

The Americans noted that Canada's northern terrain was much like that of Siberia. Would Canada, could Canada test the Cruise for the Western alliance? The proposition came at a time when Canadian-American relations were strained over the Canadian government's policies for limiting foreign investment, and its pursuit of a self-sufficient energy policy. A refusal by Canada on this issue might have repercussions in other fields. A military officer attached to the Privy Council Office explained what then happened. "I was personally very deeply involved in that. In fact I think I drafted the first memos on that," Donald Macnamara later said.

> ...Our whole negotiation in relationship with NORAD, and the main reason that we were involved in NORAD in the defence of North America was to contribute to the defence of the credibility and response ability of the strategic deterrent that rested in the United States Cruise missile and ballistic missile force, so that we were committed to the defence of North America, to defend the deterrent. The Cruise missile was part of that deterrent force.... It made a whole lot of sense then for us to contribute to the credibility of that deterrent by contributing to the testing of the missile.... Now why should it be important for us to have the missile tested in Canada? Because, by and large, the terrain over which that Cruise missile would have been flying, in war, in an attack on the Soviet Union, was very similar to the northern part of Canada, to the Northwest Territories....[2]

There were two apparent obstacles to a positive Canadian response to Cruise testing. The first was the mobilization of a substantial body of opinion against Cruise testing. Cruise testing, especially when coupled with the belligerent impression made by the Reagan administration, awoke dormant fears of nuclear destruction in Western countries. In Germany, Great Britain, the Netherlands, Canada and even the United States, peace demonstrations broke out. Demonstrators carefully painted outlines of their imaginatively vaporized bodies on pavements, donned skull masks, and went out to do battle with their warmongering governments. Their actions were hailed by eager commentators as the dawn of a new era of people power, similar to the anti-nuclear protesters of the late 1950s or the student revolutionaries of 1968.

The activities of the peace demonstrators were skeptically viewed by the authorities they were denouncing. For one thing, the demonstrators of this renewed Peace Movement seldom mentioned the Soviet missile deployment to which the West was responding. This provoked skepticism if not outright suspicion: "Particularly interesting was the impact that other peace movements had...in Europe," one Canadian strategist recalled.

> We had virtually irrefutable evidence that this was being funded by the Soviet Union: the marching in the streets really got the attention of a lot of the Europeans and the deployment of the American Cruise missiles in Europe was considerably compromised and delayed by the effectiveness of this peace movement initiative.[3]

Trudeau, perhaps because he had once participated in such demonstrations himself, was unimpressed by the Cruise critics. He accepted that NATO's strategic position was being threatened, agreed to the Cruise tests, and bluntly explained why in the House of Commons. When he received a letter from Brezhnev that promised in effect to take Canadian targets off the Soviet Union's strike list if Trudeau would only, as the phrase went, "refuse the Cruise," the Soviets were firmly told No.

Trudeau's decision to allow testing seemed daring, flying in the face of the fashionable and respectable Left opinion that frequently supported the Liberal party. But in Canada, as in Germany, Great Britain, the Netherlands, the United States and elsewhere the Peace Movement proved to have little staying power. If anything, it drove voters out of the political centre, where they had reposed comfortably for most of the Cold War, onto the political right. Margaret Thatcher in Great Britain, Ronald Reagan in the United States, and Helmut Kohl in Germany reflected this move to the right; in power, they in turn shifted considerably the ideological balance within NATO and in the Group of Seven, the informal but perpetual grouping of the most economically significant Western countries.[4] In the annual "G-7" summits Western leaders were more inclined in the 1980s than the 1970s to a firm policy on East-West and North-South relations.

The Group of Seven gave Trudeau a forum to advance his views on foreign policy—which, apart from a relatively restrained approach to the Soviet Union based on the status quo in Europe, also involved a generous policy toward the Third World. These views were not popular with Thatcher or Reagan and contributed to a certain tension at the Group of Seven summits.

"Grade Two," Trudeau murmured to an assistant after one summit encounter with Reagan. Trudeau's harping on peaceful outcomes with the Soviet Union in turn irritated the Americans, who described his summit contributions as "tiresome."[5] Worst of all, in American eyes, was the impression that Trudeau viewed the two sides of the Cold War as "equivalent," equating the moral worth and conduct of the United States with that of the Soviet Union. For the Reagan administration, which harked back to the comfortable certainties of the 1950s, this was an intolerable affront, and an impression that Canadian diplomats in Washington worked long and hard to dispel.

But was there, after all, a serious contradiction between Trudeau's pronouncements and established Western practice? Let us take the case of Poland, which in the late 1970s was the home of a lively and democratic trade union movement. Soviet intervention was threatened in uneasy Poland in 1980-1 and the Communist government there finally proclaimed martial law. Trudeau made it plain in public that martial law was Poland's business, not his. In private he consulted with the Germans to see whether they could together help formulate a sensible Western response. No other Western government, he found, was prepared to do more at the time, agreeing with Canada that martial law imposed by a Polish government was better than an invasion by the Soviet Union.[6]

The Soviet Union shifted uneasily in the face of the Western response to the emplacement of the SS-20, and American rearmament. The Soviet government had been assured by its intelligence organization, the KGB, that the Peace Movement would prevail. It was severely disillusioned when the movement failed and the Cruise missiles were tested and emplaced. The Soviet government also apparently believed that with Reagan's election war had become more likely and at several points between 1981 and 1983 Western activity sparked near-panic in Moscow. At one point Moscow seems to have mistaken

NATO military exercises for a prelude to war, and NATO troop movements had to be scaled down in order to reassure the Russians that the apocalypse was not, after all, around the next corner.

The real problem for the Soviet Union was that the failure of the Peace Movement left it with no real policy in dealing with the West. At the same time, oil prices were collapsing, reducing Soviet revenue from abroad, and the latest generations of American weaponry were proving painfully superior to anything the Soviets could produce. The aging Brezhnev retreated into a cocoon of ill health, surrounded by almost equally elderly retainers who themselves took refuge behind a shield of rigidity. Brezhnev's death in 1982 did not improve matters: his chosen successor, Yuri Andropov, was in the last stages of kidney disease and spent his brief months in power attached to a dialysis machine.

It was under Andropov that the next great crisis of the Cold War occurred. A Korean airliner, flight KAL 007, veered off course en route from Anchorage, Alaska, to Seoul, Korea, and flew over Soviet territory. After some confusion, Soviet fighters shot down the Korean plane, killing all 269 aboard, including 9 Canadians. The reaction of the rest of the world was shock; the reaction of the Soviet leadership was first denial and then the claim that the aircraft's course was somehow deliberate and that it must have been on some kind of spy mission. For Ronald Reagan, who had dubbed the Soviet Union an "evil empire," the KAL 007 incident was proof positive of Soviet barbarism and irresponsibility. Cold War exchanges sank to new depths.

In Ottawa, Prime Minister Trudeau decided that it was urgent that he act to try to defuse the situation. Already deeply mistrustful of American leadership, and influenced by the opinions of several prominent advocates of nuclear disarmament, Trudeau launched in the fall of 1983 what came to be called his "peace initiative" during which he visited several Eastern and Western countries trying to persuade them to encourage the US and the Soviet Union to negotiate a reduction in the number of nuclear weapons and to discuss ways the tension in the Cold War could be lessened.

His initiative was a hard sell, perhaps hardest on the Soviet side where there was literally no-one to listen and where Trudeau was unable to secure an appointment to see the dying Andropov. He toured the capitals of Eastern Europe where the SS-20s were located, and in each country officials dutifully lined up on the tarmac to greet the touring Canadian. ("Why is he here?" one puzzled Czech diplomat whispered to a Canadian colleague. The Canadian had no answer.)

It was certainly no joy-ride for Trudeau. He had to interview Margaret Thatcher, who detested his liberal opinions, domestic and foreign, and by extension his mission, which she thought compromised a policy of Western firmness behind the United States. Trudeau went to see India's Indira Gandhi, who was busy creating her own nuclear deterrent for local, South Asian use. He visited China in the depths of winter, and exchanged cordialities. Finally, Andropov's death allowed a visit to Moscow for the funeral and a brief chat with Andropov's successor, the uncomprehending Konstantin Chernenko.

In the midst of all this Trudeau visited Ronald Reagan to try to persuade him of the bona fides of his mission. But since the mission suggested that Trudeau distrusted American leadership—and since Trudeau's opinion of Reagan was moderately well known—Reagan's assistants were not prepared to make the usual rhetorical bows toward their good neighbour Canada. Trudeau must have been smoking something, one senior American diplomat told a Washington dinner party. As for the actual discussions with Reagan, one American present found them patronizing on Trudeau's part. The Americans responded with a lecture on the realities of the Cold War and geopolitics.

And then he was gone. At the end of February 1984 Trudeau announced his retirement from politics. In June he handed over the Liberal succession and the prime ministership to John Turner, a former finance minister and no admirer of Trudeau's, and departed. The Soviet reaction is unknown; perhaps given the vacuum at the heart of Soviet politics there was none. The American reaction is known: "We put up with Trudeau for so long," one official said. Anything, presumably, would be better.

Brian Mulroney, Defence and Foreign Policy

Trudeau's successor, Turner, did not have the chance to be anything much. He led a doomed party into an electoral slaughter in September 1984, surviving personally to be Leader of the Opposition until 1990.

The victor in the 1984 elections was quite a different species from Trudeau. Brian Mulroney was a Montreal lawyer, labour specialist, and corporate executive. He was known to be an enthusiast for the United States, and he had already made a trip to Washington to introduce himself to Ronald Reagan and his administration. Though the Americans did not take sides between Mulroney and Turner, they had reason to be pleased with the Canadian electorate's choice.

Americans like to regard Canada as their closest ally; Mulroney was determined to live up to expectations. Unlike Trudeau, where the Cold War was concerned, Mulroney stood with Reagan. At the Group of Seven, the Canadian voice sang a different song. And at gatherings all over the world Mulroney defended the United States and its president. He was not displeased that word of his pro-American disposition and comments got back to Washington, where Reagan came to regard him as a true friend.

Such an approach had its advantages. Trudeau was a burden to be endured for the American president. Mulroney on the other hand was an experience to be savoured, and repeated. Reagan took pleasure in Mulroney's company, and in reports that Mulroney in his trips around the world was lavishing praise on the United States and its leader. No equating the United States and the Soviet Union here—another relief after the carping Trudeau. Mulroney for his part believed that his cultivation of Reagan conferred advantages on Canada and ensured that his country got special and favourable consideration; and sometimes he was right.

Mulroney moved to increase, modestly, Canada's armed forces. That was an issue on which Conservatives were generally agreed: 72 per cent of delegates at the Conservative convention that chose Mulroney as leader pronounced themselves in favour of increased defence spending; 68 per cent wanted to increase Canada's role in NATO; and 74 per cent favoured testing the Cruise missile.[7] Polls, however, showed something else: rank and file Conservatives were not nearly as enthusiastic as convention delegates to seek a stronger defence or align Canada more closely with its NATO allies. Under the circumstances, Mulroney and his ministers may have got something of a mixed message from their supporters.[8] The garrison in Europe was reinforced, but not to the extent of reversing the cuts made by Trudeau in 1969. The government authorized a defence review and talked grandly of purchasing nuclear submarines. The defence review, when it reported in 1987, confirmed that Canada's military could not "fully and effectively" meet the country's commitments. Perhaps Mulroney would take the necessary steps? There was a brief boom in defence lobbying in Ottawa as foreign contractors prepared competitive bids.

It was, in the end, all for naught. Mulroney was more constrained by the Trudeau legacy than he originally imagined. Trudeau had not, after all, actually withdrawn from NATO, and in the early 1980s he had even authorized some fairly significant equipment purchases, such as the CF-18 fighter. But for the most part, the money that had once been spent on the military was by the 1980s irretrievably committed to Canada's social programs, a legacy of the 1960s that Mulroney, sensitive to the wishes of the electorate, described as a "sacred trust." Canada could do a little rejigging of its commitments, and fiddle at the margins of military expenditure, but the country was in a budgetary bind.

The 1987 defence review identified four main tasks for Canada's defence forces: strategic deterrence, conventional defence, protection of sovereignty, and peacekeeping. Peacekeeping—which that year involved some 900 Canadian troops scattered across the face of the globe—was generally considered a "soft" activity, an example of international do-goodism. To some extent it was, tapping the rich vein of moralism and sentimentality that had characterized public life in Canada and many other places. Some support not otherwise obtainable accrued to the armed forces as a result.

Peacekeeping also had its prudential side. Trouble spots might become less troublesome, international contentions might be cauterized by an effective deployment of peacekeepers. Canadian staff officers liked to analyze international crises in terms of their ability to turn into larger conflicts—conflicts that might drag in the Western and Eastern blocs and become a threat to world peace. Peace was not quite indivisible, but its maintenance had a clear relationship to the world's strategic balance. Canada's national interest was therefore served, and by a technique that was more or less within Canada's reduced military means.

The Americans, who under Reagan let it be known that they thought Canada's military effort was insufficient and certainly not in keeping with Canada's standing as a respectable member of NATO, were disappointed. The British too were disappointed—at least their prime minister Margaret Thatcher and her associates were disappointed—that what they took to be Canadian sanctimoniousness had not been extinguished with Trudeau.

A Topsy-Turvy World: The Cold War Ends

American hopes and Canadian fears were, however, overtaken by events. The Soviet gerontocracy had finally reached its limits with the expiry of Konstantin Chernenko in 1985. Mikhail Gorbachev, who as Soviet agriculture minister had toured Canada in 1983, and at fifty-four a much younger man, succeeded as general secretary of the Communist party. Stylish, relatively open, and energetic, he was an obvious contrast to the hulking Brezhnev and his court, a contrast as well to the sinister Stalin and the unsophisticated Khrushchev.

Gorbachev was forthwith adopted by the Western media, who sensed, and hoped, that a genuine change was occurring in Moscow. Western foreign offices, including Canada's, remembering fifty years of deferred hopes, kept their powder dry. Gorbachev's photogenic style of politics exercised an irresistible attraction on his fellow politicians, at least of the Western variety. Soon Gorbachev on tour became a highly desirable commodity, strolling Ottawa's Sparks Street Mall and being mobbed by happy, starstruck citizens. Gorbachev was naturally pleased, and possibly deceived (his later career showed he was less popular than he believed), by the adulation he received. Admittedly he had other things on his mind —the Soviet Union's technological backwardness, its precarious economy, its unbalanced budget. Gorbachev's admission that there was a problem was a revolutionary act. It is not surprising that the extent of the problem and the difficulty of its solution were seriously, profoundly, underestimated.

Gorbachev brought movement to Soviet foreign policy, and flexibility. Strategic arms negotiations between the Soviet Union and the West, paralyzed for years in a political swamp and muffled in military jargon, suddenly swung into motion. Gorbachev and Reagan met in 1985, 1986 and 1987 to work out agreements to ban intermediate nuclear weapons. In 1988, Gorbachev withdrew Soviet troops from Afghanistan. In 1989-90, one after another, the cherished positions of Soviet foreign policy were abandoned, most notably the determination to hold on to Eastern and Central Europe at all costs. One after another, the leaders of the Communist states of Eastern Europe were told that next time there was a problem or political disturbance, the Red Army would not be there to back them up. One after another, the East European Communist governments crumbled. In November 1989 a fascinated and disbelieving West watched on television screens as West Germans, often using just their hands and sledgehammers, began to tear down the Berlin Wall brick by brick as East German border guards stood by watching. Some Communists were more adept than others at saving themselves, at taking on a democratic colouration. But most went directly into the discard bin and in some cases speedily into prison. Only in Romania was the dictatorship liquidated by violence; only in Yugoslavia did communism give way to civil war, leading inevitably to another Canadian participation in a peacekeeping mission—the first of the post-Cold War.

Canada was a follower rather than a leader in these events. The main action had to be between the United States and the Soviet Union, with some assistance from the principal European allies, especially Germany. But Mulroney made encouraging noises, and encouraged Reagan and his successor (in 1989) George Bush to believe that they were on the right track. As usually happened when significant events were afoot between the Soviet Union and the United States, the Russians and Americans had no particular need of interlocutors, and to his credit Mulroney did not try to be one.

Domestically, the Soviet Union itself was wound up by stages. Gorbachev introduced some reforms in his first four years, but the pace of change increased dramatically in 1989. In local elections held in March 1990, non-Communists ran for office for the first time in seven decades and won control of the city councils in Kiev, Leningrad, and Moscow. Gorbachev attempted to create a new federal structure in his country that would afford some genuine recognition of the Soviet Union's many nationalities. His efforts were repeatedly frustrated, and then side-tracked by an abortive coup d'état in August 1991 by hard-line Communists who opposed the decline of the Communist party's position and the increasingly warm relations with the West. However, reform had made too many inroads for the August coup to succeed. Muscovites took to the street to support reform and the bulk of the army refused to join the hard-liners. In the midst of the crisis Boris Yeltsin, the president of the Russian Republic who had left the Communist party in 1990 to help start a new party, emerged as the voice of reform. The coup leaders surrendered but Gorbachev's prestige did not recover from this blow. He sat out his remaining months of office not even a prisoner in the Kremlin, until finally his nameplate was removed from his door and he was told not to turn up for work.

Through the fall of 1991, the pace of change accelerated within the Soviet Union. On 8 December 1991, in an act that had been unthinkable just a year or two earlier, Boris Yeltsin and the presidents of Ukraine and Belarus met near Minsk, Belarus, to sign documents that officially dissolved the Soviet Union. The leaders took their authority from history since these republics were the founding members of the Soviet Union in 1922. On 16 December, Kazakhstan, the last Soviet republic, declared its independence.

The Soviet Empire, the Soviet Union, and the Cold War were over.

NOTES

1. Quoted in J.L. Granatstein and R. Bothwell, *Pirouette: Pierre Trudeau and Canadian Foreign Policy* (Toronto: University of Toronto Press, 1990), 200.
2. Donald Macnamara interview, 26 August 1996.
3. Ibid.
4. Established by French president Giscard d'Estaing in 1975, the Group of Seven came to include Canada at the United States' insistence in 1976.
5. Confidential interview; quoted in Granatstein and Bothwell, *Pirouette: Pierre Trudeau and Canadian Foreign Policy*, 365.
6. See on this point Tina Rosenberg, *The Haunted Land: Facing Europe's Ghosts After Communism* (New York: Vintage, 1996), 209-10. Canada did send its ambassador, along with the Australian and Swedish envoys, to confer with the leaders of the democratic trade union movement, Solidarity.
7. Martin Goldfarb and Thomas Axworthy, *Marching to a Different Drummer: An Essay on the Liberals and Conservatives in Convention* (Toronto: Stoddart Publishing, 1988), 73, 80. Conservatives, on the other hand, favoured cutting foreign aid, while Liberals generally wished to increase it.
8. Ibid., 103. Liberal delegates were also more likely than Liberal rank and file to take a favourable view of NATO and defence, but the difference was much less than among the Conservatives: ibid., 99.

Epilogue

Looking Back

Depending on how you choose to compute it, the Cold War lasted seventy-four years (the duration of the Soviet Union itself) or roughly forty-five years, from the point when the wartime allies fell out and chose to go their separate and contradictory ways—1945 or 1946 or 1947.

The Cold War was something quite specific. It was a confrontation between a particular Communist state, the Soviet Union, and its allies and the Western powers, increasingly centred on and led by the United States. It was also a clash between Communists, many of them citizens of Western countries, and anti-Communists or non-Communists. Because Communists held and did not hesitate to use the tools of totalitarianism, the Cold War sometimes appeared to be an unequal struggle between the conforming societies of the East Bloc—the Soviet Union and its followers—and the West—the United States and its friends and allies. Only late in the day did Westerners grasp that the conformity of the East masked a false order and a spurious sense of strength. Even more to the point, Communist "progress," its claim that it contributed to greater justice through an enforced equality, proved to be bogus. Compared to the unpleasant inequalities of the Communist world, the imperfections of Western societies paled just as Western weaknesses, all too apparent to Western leaders through the decades, turned out to be less, and less significant, than the deficiencies of the East Bloc.

Some forms of Communism survived the Soviet Union. China, estranged from Moscow since the late 1950s, remained nominally Communist even as its government threw itself into an orgy of capitalist production and actively promoted the inequality of rewards among its citizens—in the name of economic growth. Vietnam reaped the harvest of its decades of revolutionary struggle by maintaining a proletarian dictatorship; simultaneously, Vietnam figured in the 1990s as a state where corruption and especially bribe-taking flourished. North Korea became a kind of hereditary monarchy that Louis XIV would have envied. It became a by-word for militarism and starvation. Cuba under its Communist dictator Fidel Castro lingered on as a kind of museum society—old cars, old doctrines, and old leaders. For most of the 1990s these countries furnished the world with a handy, visible and tangible representation of why communism had failed. The Cubans at least had their followers in Canada, and many Canadians enjoyed the inexpensive vacations that underdeveloped Cuba made possible for Western tourists clutching American dollars.

On the Western world's campuses and other unworldly sites the memory of communism lingered on, as scholars fought and refought the facts and counter-facts of the Communist era. One bizarre grouplet in Canada actually called itself "the Bolshevik tendency" in the early 1990s, and there were similar sentimental sects elsewhere in the Western world. Admittedly it was more difficult than before to argue the case for communism, for not only did the Communist image labour under the burden of failure, it had to contend with a rush of revelation from the archives of the ex-Soviet Union and its former satellites. Scholars who before were resigned to an eternally one-sided research career could suddenly compare Western impressions with their Soviet originals.

Hindsight, in the case of the Cold War, is not very old. As history goes, the Cold War is very recent, and much remains secret in the hands of governments that have an interest in obscuring or protecting past errors. But secrets sometimes have the effect of obscuring the obvious. The main lines of Canada's participation in the Cold War have been clear virtually since the beginning. A Western, liberal society, with a capitalist free enterprise economic system, Canada as it existed in the 1940s was naturally incompatible with a regulated dictatorship like the Soviet Union. When the Soviet Union showed signs of hostility (as in the Gouzenko affair) or indicated that it was not content to remain inside its own borders, the Canadian government perceived a threat that was simultaneously internal and external. With the experience of the Great Depression behind it, the Canadian government bolstered its internal defences, through a policy of social welfare, and, with the experience of the Second World War fresh in people's minds, it reinforced its external ramparts, through a policy of alliances and military commitments.

Some Canadian leaders, like Lester Pearson, understood that the Cold War was something for the long haul. That fact presented a challenge to leadership, as Pearson saw it, an expensive and dangerous commitment to an anti-Communist coalition and, moreover, a commitment of indefinite duration. For Canada the task was complicated by the facts of life of a small power, easily taken for granted by its larger partner, the United States, which in any case heavily influenced Canadian ways of looking at the world. Sometimes, and as a result, Canadians saw a contradiction between their physical security, symbolized by Canada's Cold War alliances, and their political security, symbolized by the need to keep a certain distance from their closest allies, the Americans. All Cold War Canadian governments confronted this paradox from time to time, from Mackenzie King, hanging back over the Berlin Blockade in 1948, to Brian Mulroney, lingering behind Ronald Reagan's Star Wars crusade in the 1980s.

As it happened, the period of the Cold War saw a rough balance between the concerns of Canadian sovereignty and the needs of Canadian security. In the relative stability of a near-fifty years confrontation, Canadian sovereignty found a purpose and a definition, as part of a large cause and a big alliance. The Cold War gave Canada a place that was never a mystery, though it was occasionally in question. The end of the Cold War, by contrast, forced Canada and its citizens to conceive new roles in a different world. In the late 1990s they were still wondering what role, and in which world.

RB
November 1997

Further Readings

The literature on the Cold War is vast. Most of it is obsolete, interesting only as mood- or mind-setters for specialist students of the period. With the passage of time, the tons of speculation about the Soviet Union, disguised as "social science" or "strategic studies," will give way to reliable history. A beacon for students is the splendid Cold War History Project from the Woodrow Wilson Center for Scholars in Washington, which has already extended our understanding of Soviet-Chinese relations, and the outbreak of the Korean War, and a thousand other topics.

Canada's side of the Cold War is studied almost entirely by Canadians. Aspects of the period may be captured in the standard biographies of the period. Mackenzie King was his own best biographer, and the two volumes (3 and 4) of *The Mackenzie King Record* (Toronto: University of Toronto Press, 1968, 1970) that cover 1945 to 1948 repay perusal. The biography of Louis St. Laurent is less informative and indeed quite pedestrian (Dale Thomson, *Louis St. Laurent: Canadian* [Toronto: Macmillan, 1967]). Diefenbaker requires at least two books: H. Basil Robinson's excellent *Diefenbaker's World* (Toronto: University of Toronto Press, 1989) and Denis Smith's splendid biography, *Rogue Tory* (Toronto: Macfarlane Walter & Ross, 1995). John English's two books on Lester Pearson are a definitive account of the Cold War as seen by its principal Canadian practitioner (*Shadow of Heaven* [Toronto: Random House Canada, 1989] and *The Worldly Years* [Toronto: Knopf Canada, 1992]). Trudeau's sixteen years as an extra in the Cold War drama are discussed in J.L. Granatstein and R. Bothwell, *Pirouette: Pierre Trudeau and Canadian Foreign Policy* (Toronto: University of Toronto Press, 1990). There is as yet no strong account of Brian Mulroney and certainly none that illuminates his foreign policy.

For some of the Cold War *The Canadian Annual Review* is a useful summary (for the period 1960-89 as of 1997). The *Documents on*

Canadian External Relations published by the Department of External Affairs (now Department of Foreign Affairs and International Trade) are extremely valuable, but as of 1997 they were published only down to 1954. They can be supplemented by the American collection, *Foreign Relations of the United States,* which recently reached the late 1960s. *Canada in World Affairs,* the Canadian Institute of International Affairs' survey of foreign policy, is of variable quality, but always repays reading. It came to an end with a volume covering 1969-71.

Index

116